TIMING
TIME MANAGEMENT ON STEROIDS

by LINKED IN AND TOWN HALL ACHIEVER OF THE YEAR
EY NOMINEE ENTREPRENEUR OF THE YEAR
GRAND HOMAGE LYS DIVERSITY
WORLD TOP100 DOCTORS

Dr. BAK NGUYEN, DMD

&

WILLIAM BAK

TO ALL THOSE LOOKING TO MAKE THE MOST
OF EACH MINUTE OF EACH DAY AND
TO KEEP IT GOING DAY AFTER DAY

by Dr BAK NGUYEN

Copyright © 2021 Dr. BAK NGUYEN

All rights reserved.

ISBN: 978-1-989536-79-7

Published by: Dr. BAK PUBLISHING COMPANY
Dr.BAK 0074

DISCLAIMER

« The general information, opinions and advice contained in this medium and/or the books, audiobooks, podcasts and publications on Dr. Bak Nguyen's (legal name Dr. Ba Khoa Nguyen) website or social media (hereinafter the "Opinions") present general information on various topics. The Opinions are intended for informational purposes only.

No information contained in the Opinions is a substitute for an expert, consultation, advice, diagnosis or professional treatment. No information contained in the Opinions is a substitute for professional advice and should not be construed as consultation or advice.

Nothing in the Opinions should be construed as professional advice related to the practice of dentistry, medical advice or any other form of advice, including legal or financial advice, professional opinion, care or diagnosis, but strictly as general information. All information from the Opinions is for informational purposes only.

Any user who disagrees with the terms of this Disclaimer should immediately cease using or referring to the Opinions. Any action by the user in connection with the information contained in the Opinions is solely at the user's discretion.

The general information contained in the Opinions is provided "as is" and without warranty of any kind, either expressed or implied. Dr. Bak Nguyen (legal name Dr. Ba Khoa Nguyen) makes every effort to ensure that the information is complete and accurate. However, there is no guarantee that the general information contained in the Opinions is always available, truthful, complete, up-to-date or relevant.

The Opinions expressed by Dr. Bak Nguyen (legal name Dr. Ba Khoa Nguyen) are personal and expressed in his own name and do not reflect the opinions of his companies, partners and other affiliates.

Dr. Bak Nguyen (legal name Dr. Ba Khoa Nguyen) also disclaims any responsibility for the content of any hyperlinks included in the Opinions.

Always seek the advice of your expert advisors, physicians or other qualified professionals with any questions you may have regarding your condition. Never disregard professional advice or delay in seeking it because of something you have read, seen or heard in the Opinions. »

ABOUT THE AUTHORS

From Canada, **Dr. BAK NGUYEN**, Nominee Ernst and Young Entrepreneur of the year, Grand Homage Lys DIVERSITY, LinkedIn & TownHall Achiever of the year and TOP 100 Doctors 2021. Dr Bak is a cosmetic dentist, CEO and founder of Mdex & Co. His company is revolutionizing the dental field. Speaker and motivator, he wrote 72 books over 36 months accumulating many world records (to be officialized). His books are covering:

- **ENTREPRENEURSHIP**
- **LEADERSHIP**
- **QUEST OF IDENTITY**
- **DENTISTRY AND MEDICINE**
- **PARENTING**
- **CHILDREN'S BOOKS**
- **PHILOSOPHY**

In 2003, he founded Mdex, a dental company upon which in 2018, he launched the most ambitious private endeavour to reform the dental industry, Canada wide. Philosopher, he has close to his heart the quest of happiness of the people surrounding him, patients and colleagues alike. In 2020, he launched an International collaborative initiative named **THE ALPHAS** to share knowledge and for Entrepreneurs and Doctors to thrive through the Greatest Pandemic and Economic depression of our time.

In 2016, he co-found with Tranie Vo, Emotive World Incorporated, a tech research company to use technology to empower happiness and sharing. U.A.X. the ultimate audio experience is the landmark project on which the team is advancing, utilizing the technics of the movie industry and the advancement in ARTIFICIAL INTELLIGENCE to save the book industry and to upgrade the continuing education space.

These projects have allowed Dr Nguyen to attract interests from the international and diplomatic community and he is now the centre of a global discussion in the wellbeing and the future of the health profession. It is in that matter that he shares his thoughts and encourages the health community to share their own stories.

"It's not worth it go through it alone! Together, we stand, alone, we fall."

Motivational speaker and serial entrepreneur, philosopher and author, from his own words, Dr Nguyen describes himself as a dentist by circumstances, an entrepreneur by nature and a communicator by passion.

He also holds recognitions from the Canadian Parliament and the Canadian Senate.

From Canada, **William Bak**, is a 10 years old prodigy. At the age of 8 years old, he co-wrote a series of chicken books with his dad, Dr. Bak. Together, they are changing the world, one mind at a time, writing books for kids. So far, they have 28 books together.

He co-wrote the 11 chicken books in ENGLISH and then, had to translate his own books in FRENCH. This is how he has 22 chicken books. William also co-wrote 2 parenting books with his dad, Dr. Bak, THE BOOK OF LEGENDS volumes 1 and 2. Volume 3 is in production. 2 Vaccine books (French and English) and TIMING, William first Apollo Protocol book.

To promote his books, William embraced the stage for the first time in 2019 talking to a crowd of 300+ people. Since, he has appeared in many videos to talk about his books and upcoming projects.

In the midst of COVID, he got bored and started his YOUTUBE CHANNEL : GAMEBAK, reviewing video games.By the end of 2020, he has joined THE ALPHAS as the youngest anchor of the upcoming world project COVIDCONOMICS in which he will give his perspective and host the opinions of his generation.

> "I will show you. I won't force you. But I won't wait for you.
> - William Bak and Dr. Bak

Writing with his Dad, William holds world records to be officialized:

- The youngest author writing in 2 languages
- Co-author of 8 books within a month
- The first kid to have written 24 children books

TIMING

TIME MANAGEMENT ON STEROIDS
by Dr BAK NGUYEN & WILLIAM BAK

INTRODUCTION
BY Dr BAK NGUYEN

TIME ZONES
CHAPTER 1 - Dr. BAK NGUYEN

TOOLS OF PRODUCTIVITY
CHAPTER 2 - Dr. BAK NGUYEN

STRUCTURE
CHAPTER 3 - Dr. BAK NGUYEN

TEMPLATES
CHAPTER 4 - Dr. BAK NGUYEN

THE GAMER MENTALITY
CHAPTER 5 - Dr. BAK NGUYEN

DISTRACTION
CHAPTER 6- Dr. BAK NGUYEN

SYNERGY
CHAPTER 7 - Dr. BAK NGUYEN

ON STEROIDS
CHAPTER 8- Dr. BAK NGUYEN

CONCLUSION
BY Dr. BAK NGUYEN

GLOSSARY OF Dr. BAK's LIBRARY
ANNEX - Dr. BAK NGUYEN

10

INTRODUCTION
by Dr. BAK NGUYEN

You know that I'm writing books. I just finished my 97th but since there are two books that will not be ready on time, **COVIDCONOMICS** and **CRYPTOCONOMY**, I will have to make up for those too. So mostly I have five books left to write and I have 22 days to do so.

That's an average of 4.4 days to write a book. Last year, I had to write a book every 8 days for 8 straight weeks to set a new world record, 72 books written within 36 months. This year, the bar is a little higher.

To be honest, I don't know if I can make it. Well, I know that I can produce, to keep the pace up is the main challenge, while still writing quality content.

> "Pace and leverage will be the key to keep moving up in this kind of challenge."
> Dr. Bak Nguyen

That's quote #2468.

The timing was wrong, but in the middle of all of this, Tranie, my best friend and life partner, made me leave for 10 days of vacation. I did not write a single word within that time, shooting and travelling for **COVIDCONOMICS** (my version of vacations), until the last morning before check-in out of the hotel for the airport.

10 days later, I wrote and published the first 4 volumes of the **SHORTCUT franchise**, 4 volumes! How is that for time management? That's an average of 2.5 days per book, written and published! How cool is that?

So no, the abilities that you will learn in this journey are not the usual *time management skills*. I will teach you to **leverage** instead of to manage. How is that for a deal?

> "Time management is not about managing time, more about managing results and expectations."
> Dr. Bak Nguyen

That's quote #2469.

This is a much-needed break. With 5 of the 8 volumes of the **SHORTCUT** series written and published at a world record pace and as a personal fastest, I am making History, once more.

Since the last 2 weeks, I wrote and published 5 of the 8 volumes of the series, not only compiling the quotes of my entire library but also covering in-depth in 77 famous quotes of mine.

The first 4 volumes, **HEALING**, **GROWTH**, **LEADERSHIP**, and **CONFIDENCE** took 2 days and a half each. By the 3rd day, they were distributed by Apple Books, Amazon, and shortly after, Barnes and Noble.

I will like to take a minute to thank these big three, they are not just partners but have been my biggest and most loyal fans. When you write books at my pace, partially confined, you do not have the opportunity to meet and talk with the people you touched.

Writing at this Olympic pace, one book after the next, fatigue is not a menace but a companion. You just have to deal with it. Fatigue I know, but with my guard down, it is doubt that is growing. And that's bad!

Will I make it? Am I falling behind schedule? I don't know if I can keep it up. Running a sprint, your mind does not have the time to react and to second guess yourself. Running a *marathon of sprints*, well, your body is tired and since the delays are days and weeks, not seconds, your head has a chance to catch up. And here comes doubt.

> "Doubt has nothing to do with a lack of confidence. It is just a virus of the mind, an opportunistic infection that will flourish as you are weakened."
> Dr. Bak Nguyen

That's quote #2470.

Unless you are just weak, which in this case, doubt will take over permanently, doubt is passing like a common cold. You will heal from it. That said, I have no time to slow down, left alone, to be sick.

I still have 5 books to write and 22 days to do so. That's 4.4 days per book. That's a little less than my previous odds with 4.5 days per book. I know exactly what happened, the last one, **SHORTCUT volume 5, SUCCESS** was not a harder one to write, I just lost my momentum, a little bit of my momentum.

Writing that 5th volume took 6 days. I have excuses, of course. I was working in clinic for 2 days. But I am Dr. Bak, I do never have excuses. Then, I still took another 4 days (for a total of 6) to complete the book compared to the

2.5 days of its predecessors. Well, I wasn't feeling it. I slowed down and I had a hard time motivating myself.

> "Make a mistake and you will have to get back on track. Lose your momentum, that might be your greatest mistake, one much harder to get back from."
> **Dr. Bak Nguyen**

That's quote #2471.

I know that and I am trying my best to stay focus and to keep pushing but I can feel it, I have lost my connection with the Universe. I still managed to finish strong. I wasn't worried about finishing that book, I was worried about how to start the next one!

And this is the next one. This is when and where I need and look for support. Well, I found that support within my family with Tranie and William, my closest allies.

Right behind them, Apple Books stand, often the first to join the celebration with the distribution of that book in 51 countries. Usually, Amazon follows closely behind, a few hours later, in both formats, Kindle and Paperback.

Within the last weeks, Barnes and Noble joined the vibes of the celebrations within hours too. This is my system of support. Without them, **fatigue** and **doubt** will have eaten me alive by now. I thank and love you, my family, my partners.

Enough of the drama and lamentation. We still have a book to travel, a great journey to write together. But I need this pause! Maybe not a pause but a break from the well-oiled routine and recipe of the **SHORTCUT franchise**. I need to break from the routine and go wild. The last time, it brought my score to 2.5 days per book!

Going wild here may not be the wisest thing to do as I am in the middle of setting the next world record. So it came to me, how about breaking the habits and the routine while accelerating? I will be taking a break of a few days from the **SHORTCUT Franchise** and from my own performance. Can I do even better?

> "I don't like to manage time.
> What I know is to leverage time."
> Dr. Bak Nguyen

That's quote #2472.

So today, for the first time in my history, I will utilize the **APOLLO protocol** to write a book from an interview. I am hoping to write this book, **TIMING, Time Management on Steroids**, within a day or two. Doing this, I will usually ask Brenda or Jonas to step in, but Brenda is now in France.

I will be having an interview with Jonas in two days, this Wednesday, but by then, this book has to be done and available already. So I called for my secret weapon, my ally, he who pushed me to break the **sound barrier**, William Bak, my son.

William will be stepping in as host and will be bouncing my answers to squeeze the juice out of me, and the subject is one that I have been postponing for months by now, Time management.

Haven't I said that I do not like to manage? What I know is to leverage. More than sharing in the midst of my **100 books challenge**, the doubt, the stress, and the emotions, William and I will be pushing a notch further.

This recorded session of **Apollo protocol** is streaming live on social networks, just to keep us on our toes and to share with you without filter the coming of a new book and how it feels like to be running my challenges.

> "I found my momentum changing my wording.
> I leverage, I do not manage."
> Dr. Bak Nguyen

That's quote #2473.

This will be a chance for me to regroup and to redeploy, writing my first book thanks to the **APOLLO protocol**, to write from a camera instead of writing from my keyboard. The process is well proven and I offered that means to a few of my co-authors. Until now, I used it to prepare, prior to writing.

To write **TIMING, TIME MANAGEMENT ON STEROIDS** within one day, utilizing the power of the **APOLLO protocol**, this is great timing and steroids. Wish me luck! The routine is definitively broken!

This is **TIMING, TIME MANAGEMENT ON STEROIDS** for Million Dollar Mindset. Welcome to the Alphas.

> "To solve time management in four single words:
> Get rid of procrastination."
> Dr. BAK NGUYEN

CHAPTER 1
"TIME ZONES"
by Dr. BAK NGUYEN

I don't like to manage. All those who know me know that I hate to manage. What I am good at is to leverage and to win. This is the steroids part of the title. I will show you before the end of this book to layer and to leverage with William. And what about my days, how does that translate in everyday life?

Until lately, I woke up around 4 AM without alarm. At the dawn of the day, that's me at my best. It is quiet, you have all the time in the world and everything seems possible. I wake up, hit the shower, brush my teeth, and the rest of the morning, until 7 or 7:30 AM, it is mine to write.

It's the best time of the day because you're fresh and since the day has not started yet, clarity is right in reach. You know, all that noise in the day filtering you from reality, all of that is still asleep. Even part of my brain is still asleep. I don't know how to explain it, but in the morning, as I am still half asleep, this is where I have full access to my being, body, mind, and soul.

Some will say that I am in a sort of **trance**, I won't disagree. As my logic is not fully operational yet, it is my best time to assert what I did yesterday and where I am going today and tomorrow. This has also proven to be the best time for me to access and leverage my creativity.

These 2 morning hours are the equivalent of maybe 6 hours of productivity in a normal day because I am unfiltered and not disturbed.

I've come to treasure that time. That's my me time, meditating as I am writing and sharing with you. It is also where everything, past, present, and future make sense of everything.

Lately, because of COVID, it has been harder to keep that serenity and that routine. Fatigue, frustration, and late-night TV shows have somehow disturbed my temple. Oh, that's no excuse, I am still producing and accelerating the pace. But that is what also explaining why I have to write as much as fast now to set the next world record.

> "If you try to achieve anything of worth, consistency is the key."
> Dr. Bak Nguyen

That's quote #2474.

Well, like they say, you don't have to be great to start, you just need to start to be great! This is about action and consistency.

So about when is the right time? The answer is always **NOW**! Now is the time to move forward. Yesterday could have been better, but thinking of that, you are wasting even more of **NOW** and will set both your feet deep in regrets. Pretty intense to free yourself from there. So why do that to yourself, **NOW** is always your right answer.

Do it NOW, so you free TOMORROW
For better, for more.
Do it NOW, so you can build on top
And ladder your way up.

Do it NOW, so you can move on
With the confidence that you've done it.
Do it NOW, that's the best favour
You are gifting yourself with.

Today, I sometimes walk up at 7 AM, even 8. That is not my typical day, but it is me falling victim to the pressure of COVID.

> "COVID did not attack my body, it attacked my spirit, and my body suffered as collateral damage."
> Dr. Bak Nguyen

That's quote #2475.

And, do I have to say it? I am not a victim! COVID is killing my vibe. Is this the best timing to challenge the world with records?

> "It is the best time to do so.
> Why, because it is NOW!"
> Dr. Bak Nguyen

That's quote #2476.

This is me fighting back. I fell asleep at the wheel and now, I am playing catchup. Is that the best strategy? Well, that's what I have, **NOW**! That's my timing.

Easier said than done. Consuming, you are setting your body and hormones in a different state. Somehow, you are producing less vital energy and you are starting to grow roots. From there, your body will have changed 90 degrees and your hormonal response is not the same anymore.

Why is this so important? Because you are what you feel! And whatever you think and believe, you will produce the associate hormones **to prove you right**! You will be experiencing physically your beliefs. This is how the body works.

You don't believe me? Well, in medicine, there is a very well-known phenomenon called the placebo effect. The placebo effect will cause one to die from poison even if what he or she has ingested were sugar and food colorant.

If you think that you are sick, you will feel sick, soon enough, because your body will be producing hormones that will trigger the same reactions and sensations as if you were sick.

Did you know that most of the pain and side effects we are experiencing from an illness, poison, a virus, the worse is often relate more to how our body reacts versus the attack itself? Now, you understand how powerful can the placebo effect be.

So back to my morning, well, it is the best time because, for once, I am not playing catch up. I am free to do and feel what I want, what I feel at that present moment. Because it is so early in the morning and that most people are sleeping, I do not feel that I have started my day yet.

To me, it seems like cheating, finding extra time to train, to share, to win.

This also produces a great feeling of accomplishment as I greet the rest of the world at 8. As they are waking up, I have already achieved something. That great feeling set my day on a great path, with hormones of endorphins.

Ever try morning sex? People say that it is a great way to start your day. Try waking up at 4 and perform at your best. You will have top even sex! Did I just said that?

So morning is the best time of the day, productively. Then after that, just like everybody, I have to face my usual as a doctor, a father, a CEO, a husband, a son. The leverage that I have is going through all of those with the **leftover endorphins** and sometimes, adrenaline I had from my morning sessions (and I am not talking about sex here).

To be honest, from 8 AM to 8 PM, the day is not mine. It's the flow of life running and I'm happy conforming. Usually, after dinner and a shower, it is also a great time to sit down and relax.

Will I be turning the TV on or my computer on? One I will be consuming, the other I will be producing. I do as I feel.

It's often 50-50. 50% of the time, I will be watching TV and falling asleep on the couch after the first few minutes. That is great since I will be back up at 4 AM to be at my best.

The other 50% of the time, I will be sitting at my home office and responding to my day and what happened. I usually am not as productive and creative than I would be in the early morning, but it is also the best time for me to start prepping my books and chapters.

Usually, this is when I will be making my book covers (before even writing the first words). This is when I would be upgrading my personal website and sharing posts on social media. This is also when I would be preparing my to-do list for tomorrow. This is my prep time.

If I have published a book on Apple Books today, well, the evening is also when I will be finishing the editing and formatting to submit to Amazon and Barnes and Noble. I try not to do too much creative work by night. It is just not coming as strong nor as great. But for prep work, that is the best time.

Since COVID, I spend more time at home, working remotely. I am as productive in the morning and in the evening. In between, that's another story. After lunch, that is my worse time, impossible for me to write a single word. It's just a black-out period for the following hours.

> "Don't knock your head against the wall, falling asleep."
> **Tranie Vo**

That's the kindness and wisdom of my best friend and life partner, Tranie Vo. She told me to stop torturing myself trying to go against my own body. Don't try to make the most of everything, you have nothing to prove. You know, you're capable of doing great things, but you need to set yourself up to do those and to enjoy the process. In a word, she surgically removed the guilt out of me.

My father used to teach me that if there is still a minute, I have to make the most out of it. When you are producing, you feel guilty if we stop, but that's not the idea.

The idea is to keep scoring, not just to produce but to score, and you want to **score** high. You want to do things that are haven't done before. You have to set yourself up for success, not for failure.

Well, when you are performing at the highest level, this is not how it works. When you are looking to be creative, that is the worst of all advice! To perform and to produce, you need to be at your best since that will paint your results.

> "Your results are simply the materialization of your state of mind and being."
> Dr. Bak Nguyen

That's quote #2477.

So if you feel like shit, don't have too much expectations for the outcome of your work, even less, creation. Thanks to Tranie, I dropped all of this flawed mindset and embrace freedom instead. I do what I feel! And since I have nothing to prove anymore, I am free and do not feel guilty.

So after lunch, if I am home, I go hit the pool, going for a walk, or even a drive. The other option for me is going for a nap. Yes, a nap!

I am lazy and I won't hide from that. But napping is not just about being lazy. As COVID happened, I started to take nap. You know, those naps that, when you were younger, you hate and your parents forced you to take.

Older, how much will we be ready to pay to have such delicatessen? Well, COVID served that opportunity on a silver plate.

So working from home, the days that I do not have clinical duties, I work from 4 in the morning. I write, produce, have my meetings. By lunchtime, I am pretty done with my day, unless there are more meetings set in the afternoon.

Lately, I am doing business with Canada, the USA Europe, and even Asia. Except for the west coast people (California), most people want to meet in the morning (eastern time). 8 AM here is 8 PM in Asia, you cannot go much later than that, talking business.

By 1 PM here, it is dinner time in much of Europe and the Europeans take their dining time very seriously. So for most parts of the world, meetings end at 1 PM.

For Canada and the USA, people are more flexible, but I have noticed that most people in executive positions love to have their meeting in the mornings too. So yes, my mornings are very busy. If I have meetings after 1 PM, it is usually because my schedule was full and that I had to fit these meetings in my day. I try not to.

So at 1 PM, my day is over. I can eat and have some air or enjoy the pool. That's in the summertime. In Montreal, summer is about 3 months of the year. The rest of the time, it is cold, raining when not covered in snow. So napping is the most common alternative. And this is one of the best things I've discovered.

> "Napping helped me to double my day."
> Dr. Bak Nguyen

That's quote #2478.

Let me explain. I told you that when I wake up in the morning, I'm feeling available and fresh, I can write. And this is how I wrote most of my books at a super hero pace. Now, after my nap, which will last for about an hour to an hour and a half, as I woke up, I had the same feeling like if it was 4 AM.

It just feels like it is a brand new day. That was a way from me to double my productivity because now I have two mornings! To be honest, it is not even close to the magic felt at dawn, but it is the closest I could recreate. Sure, I still have to share that time with the rest of life but I am at least fresh and available.

So that's my day, in zones: 4 AM morning - lunch - nap - second coming - dinner - evenings. At least, this is my day as I am working. On the weekends and on vacations, there are simply no rules, it is the **BREAKING THE HABITS** policy. Then, everything goes!

This is **TIMING, TIME MANAGEMENT ON STEROIDS** for Million Dollar Mindset. Welcome to the Alphas.

"To solve time management in four single words: Get rid of procrastination."

Dr. BAK NGUYEN

CHAPTER 2
"TOOLS OF PRODUCTIVITY"
by Dr. BAK NGUYEN

My tools of productivity are nothing out of this world. If you are talking about writing books, the tools that I'm using are pretty common: my iPhone and my MacBook pro. Combined those with a great internet connection and I can do pretty much most of my work, even dentistry!

I was doing that before COVID but as confinement hit last year, what I did to keep connection with my patients became mainstream. I can still not operate from a distance but pretty much everything else can be managed remotely. Today, half of my work as a dentist, I do remotely. And that will stay, even after COVID.

On that, zoom calls and email became a new norm. The hours in the day also are pretty flexible. I tend to prefer emails to zoom calls when it is possible. An email can be answered promptly as I have a few minutes while a zoom call is like a meeting, both parties need to be available at the exact same time. Both can be run from my iPhone and laptop.

If you are addressing my CEO position, my iPhone and laptop are 80% of my tool kit. Of course, that combined with a great and reliable internet connection. I even managed to produce and broadcast a talk show with only these tools, **THE ALPHASHOW** which now has chance to reach

Hollywood through NETFLIX/Amazon Prime. Producer Barry Rosen is working on our contract at the time of this writing.

I started with my laptop and slowly upgrade my cameras, lighting, and microphones. The main boundaries were the internet connection, its speed, and how reliable it was.

Now let address the main course of this conversation, the tools of my momentum, writing books. Well, they are the same two, my iPhone, my laptop, and an internet connection.

"Moving forward, your main enemy is procrastination."
Dr. Bak Nguyen

That's quote #2479.

I literally wrote my first few books with my iPhone 7 plus and later on, my iPhone X. I must say that I preferred by far the iPhone 7 plus since the screen was much bigger than the iPhone X.

That said, I wrote my chapters as if I was texting. I literally wrote my chapter with 2 thumbs up! Writing with my iPhone kept things simple and very casual. I wrote on the note application, native with any iPhone, nothing fancy! Then, I airdropped my "notes" into my word processor (Pages) and this is where the books start to take shape.

So I'm writing my first book, actually, it wasn't even a book. I was writing Ted talks just to get prepared to embrace the stage, scheduled to speak after Michelle Obama, the former first lady of the USA. That's how my writing career started, 4 years ago.

That promise never materialized and I never spoke after Michelle Obama yet. But I was ready. Her name and prestige put the fear of God in my heart. I was also too proud to say that I am chicken out! I utilized each free moment I had, preparing my speeches (Ted Talks), writing from my iPhone, even as I was waiting for my next patients to come.

Ted Talks became chapters and chapters became books, within days. 2 weeks to be precise. Would I be able to write as fast, having to sit down in front of a laptop? I don't think so. Fear and the accessibility of writing from an iPhone kept procrastination at bay and very soon, success followed.

On that, I still kept close to me these 2 relics, my iPhone 7 plus, and my iPhone X as they are the tools that empowered me to my rise, writing world records after world records...

> "I started making History with 2 thumbs up!"
> Dr. Bak Nguyen

That's quote #2480.

My first tool was my iPhone. Then, I kept writing more and more books. Eventually, it was time to think about having them published. By my 5th book, I received my first rejection from the publishers, the 3 biggest names of Quebec.

Being turned down is hard. I was pissed, not because of the rejection but because they took 3 months to do so. Do you know what I can do in 3 months' time? I picked myself up, swallowed my pride, and said, okay, let's do something with that.

> "If I have made it until now, it was not because I stood still, waiting for permission or approval."
> Dr. Bak Nguyen

That's quote #2481.

So I got my rejection, that's okay. If they don't want to publish me, I will publish myself. By that time, I was opening **Mdex & Co**, the new concept in dentistry. I had a whole floor of prime real estate, downtown Montreal. I am going to publish my own stuff, only not on paper!

Each meeting and operation room got named with a quote of mine. Imprinted on the doors, I leveraged my business office as a tool to publish my thoughts. That became a huge success!

As patients were flowing in, they took pictures of these quotes and posted them on their own social media. We have strangers asking to come by and to take pictures of these quotes to post on their walls. I did not sell any book, but people were posting my quotes. People were loving them! Not just my patients, people I have never met! And that was a huge boost, not just in ego, but in satisfaction.

> "Confidence is sexy."
> Dr. Bak Nguyen

That is amongst my most popular and surely my favourite. Well, my confidence pushed me to pick up the pieces and to bypass the permission process. It will take another year before I learnt to publish on Apple Books and Amazon.

By book #7, as I was defending my nomination as Ernst and Young Entrepreneur of the Year, I wrote **CHANGING THE WORLD FROM A DENTAL CHAIR**, explaining my vision and business proposal to the judges but also to my bankers, investors, and clients.

I wrote that book in 6, maximum 7 days. I had a window of 2 weeks to get it corrected, editing and printed to present it to the judges on time. I hired a publishing company. They took care of the editing and the printing. And that book became my first published book.

It came in a few hours before I had to defend my nomination in front of the judges. That was done in record time, compared to the standards of the book industry. I was pretty proud of myself.

It's a unique feeling to hold your book for the first time in your hands. This is a feeling I wish to all of you to experience one day because we each have a story worth sharing.But that came in with a considerable bill.

As I kept writing more and more books, I could not afford to pay a few grants each time. I needed a better solution. It took another 10 months before I could finally crack the format of Apple Books with the help of Brenda, my counsellor. After book #36, Apple Books became my #1 fan, making my book available internationally in 51 countries.

The first time that they approved my book, it took 30 days. Then, it went down to a week and finally, to a few hours. They were pushing my books because we worked very hard so they look good on the multiple screen sizes of iPads and iPhones.

Then, it took me another 2 months or so, to understand and crack the standards of Kindle and Amazon print on demand. Each one of them, Apple Books, Kindle, and Amazon have their own standards. It was a lot of trials and errors.

Add that workload to the duty of a doctor treating patients, a CEO challenging the status quo of his industry, and a world record author, and you will understand the pressure and workload I was burying myself with.

Please keep in mind that I was still writing a book every 2 weeks on averages, setting the world records of **36 books written within 18 months plus 1 week** and **48 books written within 24 months**. Those alone were impossible tasks.

How did I manage to achieve that much? A chapter at a time, writing casually and looking for fun and personal satisfaction. Then, publishing, I learnt to write natively from my laptop. That saved me the time to write and to format.

I was comfortable and loved my new habit, procrastination was not a problem anymore. So my MacBook Pro became my tool of predilection to write.

On my laptop, the next tool I utilized was the use of templates. Apple Books, Kindle, and Amazon, each have their own standards. After months of trials and errors, I finally find the recipe that they love. I kept them as templates.

Today, as I start a new book, well, I duplicate my latest book script and write on top of the old manuscript, making the best use of the templates that I created with experience.

> "Templates are my way to leverage the past into a stepping stone for the next."
> Dr. Bak Nguyen

That's quote #2482.

Templates will be one of my main tools as it comes to leveraging my time and expertise. How do I keep myself motivated from one book to the next? I start with my **flag**! That's my title and book cover.

Usually, the cover is the last thing on the TODO list of a writer. Not to me. It is actually the first thing that I would do, in my **prep zone time**. At first, I tried to hire artists to make my cover. It was time-consuming and frustrating.

As a movie producer, I am pretty good with graphic and design. I did not want to have yet another task but as the artists that I hired dropped the ball, I picked it up.

Today, I am making my own book covers utilizing KEYNOTE, part of the production suite of Apple with PAGES and NUMBERS. Well KEYNOTE is the equivalent of POWERPOINT, it was not designed to make books covers and yet, it has so many powerful graphic features.

I mastered and leverage all of them and today, I am a powerhouse designing books covers! Actually, I enjoyed that time building the branding of my next book. This is kind of my mental preparation time before jumping in headfirst to write, yet another book!

So my tools are mainly my creativity, my mind, my iPhone, my MacBook Pro, my cameras and microphones, a great internet connection, and my templates. Those are my armoury.

My partners and biggest fan are Apple Books, Amazon, and lately, Barnes and Noble. They are not tools, they are my support group! Without them, keeping this pace up would be much harder.

> "Moving forward, I learnt to pack light
> to keep momentum."
> Dr. Bak Nguyen

That's quote #2483.

This is **TIMING, TIME MANAGEMENT ON STEROIDS** for Million Dollar Mindset. Welcome to the Alphas.

"To solve time management in four single words:
Get rid of procrastination."

Dr. BAK NGUYEN

CHAPTER 3
"STRUCTURE"
by Dr. BAK NGUYEN

Structure is the keyword here. I love my creativity and freedom, those are there for the **FUN**. For **SPEED**, I need structure. Combine them both together and you have **MOMENTUM**.

> "FUN x SPEED = MOMENTUM and GREATNESS."
> Dr. Bak Nguyen

That's quote #2484.

I told you about the different **time zones** of my day and how different will be my task within each time zone. Well, if I want to enjoy my time writing freely in the early mornings, I need to prep at night to have the right **structure**, **map**, and **mindset**.

Structuring may sound like work but put in the right way, it is actually really, really fun! Structuring may take some time to start in the right direction but it will save you so much down the line. To me, branding is part of structuring. I do not brand to sell, I brand to motivate myself!

So usually, after a new idea flourished in my mind, the first thing that I would be doing is to play with that thought.

What is the use, who is the audience, how long it will take before I could get out of this journey, what special resources it will required, and for what impact are the questions I will be juggling with?

If the idea survives the simulation process, which takes 5 to 10 minutes, the next phase is branding. I need a catchy name, a logo (or cover), and the spine of the project (a table of content in the case of a book). Usually, I will be playing with these for a few days before making it officially into a project.

About my books and shows, I will then published their communication announcing the upcoming projects on my website and from, there, I will publish them on social media. So yes, branding and communication are the initial phases of my writing process.

I am branding to motivate myself and to have the feeling that I am walking on solid ground. I am publishing to force myself to start and for accountability. There is no way but forward for me from that point on.

"An idea is nothing but air until you start investing in it. It can be very powerful and fade within a moment."
Dr. Bak Nguyen

That's quote #2485.

I guess, the logic of my prioritization process is the empowerment of freedom to support creativity at its birth and the organization of the resources (inspiration, time, and motivation) for it advent.

In the last chapter, we addressed my tools. Well, to be honest, my real resources are **INSPIRATION**, **TIME**, and **MOTIVATION**. Inspiration, I empower with freedom. Motivation, I use, leveraging my entire body and its emotions (hormones). And Time, well, Time is given but to have any power out of it, I need a map and a way to build dam and power.

"The entirety of my prioritization and sorting process is to empower and support that formula, Inspiration, Time and Motivation."
Dr. Bak Nguyen

That's quote #2486.

So let take the books' writing as an example. I let myself run free to find the subjects and the audiences. I do not write for a specific audience, I write and will address what

I feel, see and understand. That said, I am more appealing to some people, that I am aware but this will not be a limiting factor.

Finding the title is the first stop. I need in the least amount of words possible, something catchy, something that will provoke. I like to use a bold word, like **RISING** or **HEALING**. The other option is to have a full sentence as title, like **CHANGING THE WORLD FROM A DENTAL CHAIR**. Those aren't rules but preferences and what I found to work well with me and the audiences I appeal to.

Once I have the wording right, I need to give body. I will be doing that by making the cover of the book. In the case of a company, that would be the design of the logo. Playing with the fonts, the images, and the colour palette will give you a sense of the themes and the promises of the journey ahead.

This is a crucial part because it is here that you are borrowing from others to build your own project. The fonts, the images, the palettes, I do not invent them, I seek and sort them out to reorganize them into something unique. I am very aware that I am building on the shoulders of others. I am grateful.

On my front cover, there is the title, the image, the name of the authors and contributors (I am building up my team). On the back cover, there is always a dedication, (TO ALL ...) that's to identify the audience. There is a quote that is the promise or the hypothesis of the journey ahead. And then, there is the summary of the book.

That is the first test. Can I write the trailer of my book? This is often the fun part. If I can do that within minutes with ease and fun, I know that this journey is promising. If not, I have to go back to the inspiration and creation process, something is not right yet.

As you can see, it is not simply a protocol but a creative process with fail safes built-in, one in which each step will lead to the next one, empowering and acknowledging my feelings and emotions.

> "If I don't have to think and my body is propelling me,
> I know that the idea is powerful and promising."
> **Dr. Bak Nguyen**

That's quote #2487.

After the cover, the link on my website, and the announcement of what is coming next, I am structuring my book with the table of content. In the case of my books, I came to favour 8 chapters, an introduction, and a conclusion. I discovered the number 8 writing chicken books with William. 8 is the dragon number.

My introduction is always my personal diary of what happened between the last introduction and now. All of my introductions are also repackaged to form the **POWER OF YES** franchise. And I will start any project with the introduction.

This is my acknowledgment of the past, moving forward into the future. It is also my way to start with a **BANG**! Like the James Bond movies where the first scene is an action scene. You are starting the movie with the last action scene of the previous movie. This sets the tone for what is coming next and eases you quickly into the action.

I am borrowing from that and will start my new journey with the high note from the conclusion of my last one. You are sharing with me my successes, glory and satisfaction. Then, as you are hot and inspired, it is time to talk about us, about our journey together. And this is how I will introduce the present subject, as our journey together.

I leverage from my last win to ease the new one beginning. That's a boost of energy, energy borrowed. Well, that energy will last for at least 2 to 3 chapters within the new journey.

Hot and inspired, I will jump into the writing as I feel it, usually a few hours after having written the introduction. I am enjoying my time, usually writing at the dawn of the day. I will not stop until I run out of words or of time.

I try to push in the new journey as quickly as possible before the momentum from the last victory runs out. I will try to surf that vibe as far as possible without looking to just stretch it out artificially.

This is why I need to address my audience and to find something new to share. I am not writing about the past and what I already know by heart. From the heart, I am sharing but I am also discovering and making sense of many events and clues as I lay them on paper.

This is the same phenomenon that teachers experience as they teach. They knew the facts but somehow, having to explain them, they will see clearly what before were just dots on the board. Well, as the dots are taking shape, linking the dot will be the narrative emerging.

So no, I do not plan my narrative before starting my journey. I prepare the field with themes and possibilities. I am open to follow where my creativity will lead. The better the preparation phase, the easier it will be for my mind to explore and to push the boundaries with the new dots appearing.

In this case, my mind is like an actor in a film. If the scenes are well constructed, the crops and the costumes real and successfully immersed you in that universe, you won't have to act. You are just reacting. That's preparation, cover, title, audience.

I am talking about writing books here since it is where I have successfully proven myself time and time again but I will address a business meeting with the same approach: starting with a **BANG** to ease people in and then, include them to build our journey together and how far we could go.

In a business meeting, after that I set up the table, it is even easier since it will be their time to talk. I just sit back and wait for a great idea to empower. And as soon as you are empowering someone, anyone, that person will like you! You just found a new friend!

> "My priority is to connect first!
> Friendship before business."
> **Dr. Bak Nguyen**

That's quote #2488.

And then, we reach for the moon and beyond! Back to the chapters. Embracing the dragon number and having 8 chapters per book was a question of structure. Each chapter will cover one or two themes.

The themes are from the table of content. Before starting the book, I always try to lay twice the amount of themes that I would be covering. Each morning, I will pick one or two from that list.

As I move forward, the ones that I don't pick are the ones that I have nothing intelligent to say about. You'll be surprised by the one rejected. Sometimes, the theme I taught would be the star of my journey ends up not making the cut. I learnt to stay very open to the possibilities.

> "I write what I feel, not just what I know."
> Dr. Bak Nguyen

That's quote #2489.

Advancing on the journey, it will get harder and harder to write since the best themes are gone already. That combined with the wearing off of the **borrowed momentum**, I could be facing a wall soon. This is where the dragon number helps.

By the time that I am running low in inspiration, I am at my 3rd or even starting the 4th chapter already. I just need to push a little to be above the 50% mark. Discipline and consistency will get me there, not to the end of the journey but just enough to pass the 50% mark.

As soon as I pass the 50% mark, I celebrate, half of my journey is complete! It is also there that I will make my math on how fast I travelled that journey. Usually, the stats are impressive and will boost me confidence and energy to keep going. Now, it has become a mental game, like the one the marathonians face.

I just passed the 50% mark and I celebrated to refuel in inspiration and motivation, I did that, compressing time with great stats. I am now good to push for the next 2 chapters. Chapter 5 and 6 will be the core and also the high of the journey. Not just for me but for my audience too.

To keep the engagement and the interest of my audience, I started with a **BANG** and welcomed them in, as us. Then, I slow down to introduce and to rise slowly with chapters 1 and 2. I can afford to slow down because now, I have your trust. You were asking for more after the big **BANG**!

By chapter 3, we are deep in undiscovered territories. This is why it is harder. In those chapters, we are right in the middle of our problem, and there is no mystery or denial anymore. We are facing the facts.

By chapter 5, we have passed the 50% mark. So the dark zone is between chapter 3 and 4, where it is challenging to keep up the pace. By chapter 5, we know our problem and we are now rising with a solution, not just hope.

I will *graduate* all of my audience by the end of chapter 6 to keep their interests. By then, they are not ready to leave yet. They want more and will be cheering for it, just like for a band to come back on stage for the encore. You are boosting the energy instead of dragging it.

Of course, I will return, with an encore. I like Steve Jobs' "Oh, one last thing…" Chapters 7 and 8 are about these one last thing before I wish them luck and embrace them. So chapters 7 and 8 are all about empowerment and the last pieces of advice. By the time that I hit the conclusion, my audience is hot and pumped, ready to embark on their own challenge and journey.

And that is my structure and how I prioritize my task. I use the book analogy because it is clear and well defined, utilizing the mapping of the dragon, 8 chapters. This can be applied in any era of your life.

First, have a goal (idea). Then, brand that idea with words and textures and colours (you now have a endeavour, a project). Then, share that idea with enthusiasm. Forget those who will say to not talk about your goals until they are complete. That is true in wartime and in competitions.

Even if Life is a big and never-ending race, this one, you are racing against procrastination and your past-self. To these 2, the more you believe, the better off you are. I don't know about you but to me, talking and sharing an idea is reinforcing my faith in that same idea. Believe in yourself and in your idea, everything starts from there.

I will borrow from my last win the momentum and energy to ease my way into the next journey. Respecting the number of the dragon, I know the mapping of any journey now. The mapping is not a preconceived idea of what is ahead, simply a time and motivation management tool.

I talk about building a **DAM** to find power. Well, the number of the dragon, 8 is that cookie cutter. Introduction, **BANG**! Chapter 1 and 2, easing in and presentation. Chapter 3 and 4, the dark zone. Chapter 5 and 6, the rise, the hope, and the conclusion. Chapters 7 and 8, empowerment and the "oh, one last thing…"

I will use my conclusion as a personal footnote, just like when you are coming down from the stage after a great speaking and people are approaching you to connect. The conclusion, just like my introduction is very personal, which will allow me to reinforce my connection with all of you.

> "If structure is the key to success, mapping is the key to momentum. That's how you will leverage time, by mapping."
>
> Dr. Bak Nguyen

That's quote #2490.

This is **TIMING, TIME MANAGEMENT ON STEROIDS** for Million Dollar Mindset. Welcome to the Alphas.

CHAPTER 4
"TEMPLATES"
by Dr. BAK NGUYEN

*"The longer you take to do something, the more doubt and procrastination will have time to settle in.
Go as fast as you can."*
Dr. Bak Nguyen

That's quote #2491.

The enemies are **doubt** and **procrastination**. If you ask me, that's **TIME MANAGEMENT**. And the only remedy I found of worth is **SPEED**. If you are talking about time management, speed will ease your way forward.

In the **ENERGY FORMULA**, my 53rd book, I covered that in depth. In the scope of this journey, let's focus on keeping our distance from doubt and procrastination. These 2 are from the mind and, as we now know, the mind is a slow mover.

If you move fast, the mind has no time to adapt, it kicks in panic mode and will just process the useful information to survive the journey (danger) you are in. That's not from me, that's biology 101 and the **fight or flight reflex**.

Well, our mind is deeply rooted in that **reflex of fight or flight**. Surviving the ages and evolution, the mind is pretty good at getting you out of trouble. And that's my leverage.

I am open and welcome the opportunities. In other words, I get myself in uncharted territories. I do it quickly so the mind does not have the time to regret and to doubt.

I jump in head first because this is what my heart and body (instincts) are telling me to do. Then, I am running the first miles on the initial boost of energy coming from the excitement of the new. That energy is not eternal and will wear off. By then, my mind has caught up and I will welcome it to help me solve the problem at hand. When the mind is not arguing, it is a fantastic team member and will always find a way to leverage from any situation.

That was possible because I moved fast, leaving no time for my brain to doubt and procrastinate (finding logical excuses not to do something). Instead, the only thing that my mind is seeking are solutions, creatives, and new solutions to an old problem.

Don't fool yourself, none of our problems are new. You might just be aware of their existence but they were there much before you. The problem was our denial and our ability to shield ourselves from seeing the truth. We learnt to accept and to compensate.

And what happened to a problem that is not attended for? It will eventually grow big enough for us to care. At that point, denial is not a possibility anymore. The longer you'll wait, the bigger the problem will be. It will take more time and resources to leverage yourself out of that one.

I do not stop and wish that I knew and did that yesterday either. That would be time poorly invested. I acknowledge and if I have the appropriate resources available, I tackle it, as soon as possible.

I ignored these problems voluntarily because I was not strong enough to face them, yet. They are liabilities that I will have to carry around until I have what it takes to face them.

And the day that I will leverage these liabilities that I am carrying around, that day I will have upgraded to the next level. This is what I meant by saying to leverage your liabilities to move forward.

So to keep winning, **SPEED** is the key against doubt, procrastination, and even pride. But how and where do I find my speed. Back at my 9th book, **MOMENTUM TRANSFER**, I covered that, saying that I feed my momentum with my emotions. This was to get started.

Once I am moving, I accelerate thanks to templates and mindsets. These are construction blocks that I mastered in the past and now, assemble them together to shape and ease the journey ahead.

Each template and mindset is a system within itself, often, the results of a previous journey. They are the know-how and skills left from experience. And those are my leverage. Call them mindsets, recipes, secrets, they are what they are, **templates**.

I like the word template because it opens a world of possibilities. The templates can either be from you are you can borrow it from someone else. You can forge them or simply adapt them to fit your need. They are useful and yet, flexible.

Have you ever used a template? I will ease your start and will keep you moving (with a map y default). Basically, all you have to do is to fill up the blanks. But that won't be enough.

As you are filling up these spaces, if you are open and flexible, you are growing and discovering new angles, new possibilities, new connections. And this is where, what started as a template, will become your masterpiece, your journey to your legend.

Well, templates are what will ease your way forward. Don't be afraid to copy, we all start by copying. What do you think that culture, education, and training are? Copies from the past. That was the way to start.

The problem is when the template is the whole of your journey, of you. You might have executed it with perfection, it is generic and has no depth. That was because all you did was to fill up the blanks and you never left any room to evolve from your original plan. In other words, from what you knew before starting your journey.

If you execute what you knew, you might become better at that art but your growth is pretty limited to the polishing of a skill. You have missed out on most of the fun and the wealth of that journey, stuck in your templates. I will advise caution using templates. You are borrowing and be aware of that fact.

> "Stay open and allow yourself to evolve from that template, this is where you cease to be in debt and you are creating your own wealth and possibilities."
> Dr. Bak Nguyen

That's quote #2492.

Templates are great to start but that is all that they are, the beginning. So back to my books, over time, I've built my own templates, from designing covers to the structure of my books and chapters. What I did 4 years ago, today, I have perfected. My recipe is leaner, lighter, and more efficient.

I did not spend my journey looking for a better templates, the templates became better as the results of my journeys and discoveries. Every time that I call my mind to the rescue, it is doing just that, to upgrade my templates!

My job is to find the excuse to use my templates and to destroy them on the first occasion. Then, I rebuild better, faster. With the accumulation of the journeys, the victories, and the failures, my templates became more and more complex, complete. Templates are now made with a combination of templates.

To quickly understand my point here, let's look at a musician. Musicians learn to read music with notes, a single note at a time. Then, as the musician evolve, he or she will be learning chords, an assemble of note with one dominant tone. That's basically a template. The musician will also learn arpeggio, which is a way to play the note of that chord.

If one master the chords and the arpeggio, he or she will still need to learn about the beat and style (rhythm) of a song to play. That is also another template. Combine these 3 templates together and you now know how to play music, even enjoy music as you go!

I borrow much from my musical training to build my templates and speed. Not just writing books but going through business and relationships, I love the used of templates to ease the transition.

> "Do and react to your consequences."
> Dr. Bak Nguyen

That's quote #2493.

As speed is empowered from the use of templates, I then react to the results and speed to evolve. Once again, reacting quickly before the mind can install doubt, I acknowledged what I feel and dug deeper. This is where and how I will break from the template and become genuine and authentic.

In a relationship, one can open up the conversation with a template. If he or she stays on that level, the discussion quickly will sound cheesy and boring. Open with a template and built from the vibe that you have generated. No two conversations are alike if you surf and adapt to the vibes.

And if you kept close to you to empower the other person as soon as possible, well, that person will need a pretty big excuse not to love you! Start with a bang and invite them in. Then, built with what they are bringing to the table!

That's one degree of templates. If you want another degree and example of templates, look at my books again. Not the books but the entire library. How did I manage to find so many subjects to write about?

Well, I am open and very curious, that is a start. It gave me my first 15 books. By the 15th, I was exhausted and emptied. Then William joined and we discovered the **power of franchising**, which is another kind of template.

To start and set up a franchise is no small thing. But as soon as the ingredients are in place and that you have the mapping scaled and adjusted, writing more books within a franchise has been my secret to write more and more, touching diversity of subjects, fields, expertises, and even audiences. Do you have any idea how hard it is for someone to change audience?

The **MILLION DOLLAR MINDSET** series, the **CHICKEN BOOKS**, the **BOOKS OF LEGENDS**, the **HORIZON** series, the **ALPHAS**, the **LAZY** books, and lately, the **SHORTCUT franchise** are all templates that brought me to new heights.

To me, the ability to use and leverage templates is a must to leverage time. Working with a template, you are utilizing a virtual team over time and space. If you are open and flexible, you are building on the shoulders of others.

Building from templates is also a great exercise of humility as you are reminded that even if you are looking to change the world, you do not have to reinvent the wheel at each turn.

Finally, working with a template is also your springboard to go to new heights, building from the old and proven structures into uncharted territories. It is a dance between the past and the future and you are in control of that **bridge**.

And this is the important point, templates are bridges, you still need to cross them and to build. The danger will be to be shadowed by the template and wasting everyone's time. Anybody can fill up the blanks. What new did you bring to the table?

> "Utilize the template to gain speed and to have something to react to. That point is your breakthrough."
> Dr. Bak Nguyen

That's quote #2494.

This is **TIMING, TIME MANAGEMENT ON STEROIDS** for Million Dollar Mindset. Welcome to the Alphas.

"To solve time management in four single words: Get rid of procrastination."

Dr. BAK NGUYEN

CHAPTER 5
"THE GAMER MENTALITY"
by Dr. BAK NGUYEN

> *"If you think that you are going through hell, keep pushing!"*
> Sir Winston Churchill

The title of this book is **TIMING**. When is the good time to start? Now, is your answer. We solve that early on, entering this journey together. Then, from the title, we have **TIME MANAGEMENT** and **STEROIDS**.

I shared with you my skillset on management which isn't management. I do not manage, I leverage, I am in it to win. Thanks to that mindset, I also learnt to compliment it with the following: I do not care who is right, as long as one of us is! That's my leadership style, after years of grinding and fighting.

So today, I do not care to be right, I am in it to win! Leveraging will set me on a course for a chance to win. Managing will at best, limit my exposures and downfall. I am not saying that it is not important but you can't play defence and offence, and to be great in both!n I am playing offence, I leverage.

That leaves us with **STEROIDS**. What are the steroids that I am talking about? Well, that too we covered but briefly. The **STEROIDS** are your **hormones**. In other words, they are the emotions that you are riding.

I taught you to align your emotions with your ambitions. Time and time again, I used the verb **FEELING** rather than **THINKING** or **KNOWING**.

> "If you are listening to your FEELINGS, emotions, and sensations, you are in tune with yourself. Only then, can you be in tune with the Universe."
> Dr. Bak Nguyen

That's quote #2495.

To me that is **TIMING**. Timing is about being ready and available to vibe in synergy with the frequency of the Universe. When great athletes are talking about being in the **zone**, they are in sync with the Universe.

When artists are talking about divine inspiration, if not on drugs, they are in sync with the Universe. When you feel like Superman after a victory, you are in sync with the Universe. Unfortunately, being in sync with the Universe is not a permanent status. That has to be reached and it can also be lost.

Ever heard an old-timer talking about losing his or her momentum? Well, he or she was in sync with the Universe and lost his or her connection somehow.

I am sharing this with you here and now because we have passed the **50% mark** already. We know the problems (procrastination and doubt) coming from the mind and how to address them. That was the initial plan going into this book. So now what?

How about easing your strike forward? Even if you move fast and have left doubt behind, you still need something to keep pushing. Some will go with hope, some others will go with Faith (which to me is hope wrapped with insecurity), some bet everything on themselves, talking about confidence. This is where I stood until I started writing.

Usually, I would be talking about confidence and show you how to find, empower, and leverage your confidence. This is still a subject of predilection to me. That said, since this journey is about time and steroids, I will skip forward to the point.

I will tell you to bet on yourself but not on your confidence, that is still too risky, bet on your **hormones**! And here comes the steroids part.

THE GAMER MENTALITY

Since my co-author is my son William, let engage in his world and wording. To understand the **STEROIDS** concept, we can picture it as the **GAMER MENTALITY**.

Younger, I love to go to the arcade to play video games. At first, it was the better graphics and sounds that were the main attraction. Then, as the home game consoles were getting better and better, it was about the experience. You can't duplicate the experience of driving a race car from the arcade, even with great gears at home.

Amongst these racing games, OUT RUN by Sega was a classic. Well, there a so many more, but that's the only one that I retain the name. The concept in OUT RUN is simple, you have to drive fast with minimum accidents and without being arrested. You are racing against the clock.

On the way, you have to pass the checkpoints. If you pass that checkpoint before your time runs out, more time got added to your timer and you are still alive to drive a little longer, until your reach your next checkpoint.

That's a game, a classic one. Well, I've noticed that going through Life, is very similar. We are walking our journey. Some won't be aware but the clock is ticking. The resources are what you have inside and around you. And all of these resources also come with an expiration date.

Move forward and leverage your resources before they expire. As you are moving forward, you will find more and different resources to replenish with. If you reach the checkpoint before the expiration of your actual resources, you have more to build with and to leverage from. If you do not reach that checkpoint before the expiration tag, you will have to do without the expired resources and with no extras.

Well, guess what? The goal is still the same but now, it's getting harder. The clock is still ticking and you have are not handicapped. Leverage yourself out of that one and you will have outgrown your challenge and that race. The point was not to pick a fight with everyone and everything.

So if you are looking for the best course of action, the easiest one here, is to move as fast as possible to your next win (checkpoint) and to collect your reward and extra time.

Now I know what you will tell me. That's a great concept in a game, in real life, no body is giving you anything, even if you've reached your checkpoint! Are you sure of that? Let me prove to you otherwise.

I am a doctor in dentistry, that you know. By now, you also know that dentistry is not my passion, it wasn't even my choice. My choice was to honour my immigrant parents and to get the 2 letters of D and R in front of my name.

For that, I had to go to school and performed for close to a decade. Yes, getting into dental school and graduating is not just about dental school but about the years prior to the admission too. Then, I reached the checkpoint, I got accepted.

That came with more work and study attached. But that also came with more respect and freedom from my parents. Then, I opened my horizon and acknowledged the other resources it came with: a line of credit!

I made the most of that line of credit and my newly found freedom to direct an independent movie as I was studying in dental school.

That got me to the doors of Hollywood as I was the first student (until that point) of the University of Montreal to ever deliver (direct and produce) an independent movie while at school. That is considering that they have a cinematography department and that I was a dental student!

Well, I reached my checkpoint and things open up. Later in life, I became a good and loved dentist. By then, I understood the resource and the leverage coming at each checkpoint. Well, every year, I had to submit my income tax and statement. This is usually a painful process since you are paying up what is due in taxes.

Well, that's the system in which we are living in. But coming with that statement is also the possible upgrade of my credit score and the possibility of a bigger line of credit. This is how I built my company, **Mdex & Co**. literally with nothing else than my licence and signature. By today, banks and investors have invested millions in my companies and we are still expanding! So this is my story.

If you dig a little bit, the checkpoints that I am referring to are also the checkpoints that you are crossing. Maybe faster, maybe not but still, you are crossing sooner or later. Did you collect your reward? And that was just the obvious part. Talking about **STEROIDS**, I was referring to even more power and resources! Are you ready?

What do you think happened the day that I got accepted into dental school? I celebrated and my confidence grew a little. I grew my confidence enough to be able to understand the leverage of the line of credit. Keep in mind that I am coming from an immigrant family that believes in cash, gold, and hard-earned. Credits and debts were poisonous fruits to them.

I understood their perspective but to me, **TIME** was my important resource, not money, so I was very open to listen and learn more about credit and debt.

Knowing that in our tax system, you are paying about 50% of your income in tax, do you understand that repercussion on your **TIME**? 6 months a year, you are working for the government! The more you make, the more you are taxed. There is no legal way out of that 6 months' time.

Then, I understood more about credit and debt. As you are borrowing money, that money is not taxed. Sure, you are paying interest on that loan but if you use that loan to generate money, the tax system will allow you to deduct the interests paid from the amount your taxes will be calculated on. In other words, even the interests, you are sharing them with the government, if you are in the business of generating profits.

Time-wise, that meant that I was borrowing time, twice! Let say that I am making $100 000 a year. After-tax (extremely simplified), I have $50 000 left after paying my fair share of taxes.

Now if I want to buy a building as an investment (to make money), and that building cost $200 000, I will need to work 4 years (4x $50 000) and not spend a single dime to afford that building, right?

Now, let take credit into account. If I go to the bank and borrow $200 000, it is not money that I earned, but money that I borrowed. How much of that money do I have available to invest? About 100% of that $200 000!

Since that building will be generating profit, the interest, let say 10% (which is huge) will be an expense that the government will accept as a deduction. In other words, if I am taxed at 50%, half of the 10% interest will be paid with money owed to the government otherwise.

So I have gained 4 years ahead of the guy working hard for his money before investing. The price I am paying for the "**shortcut**" is half paid by the government itself.

The building will be generating profit (unless I am a total failure as an administrator and even in that case, I could hire a professional management company which again, the fees will be split between me and the government).

For as long as I am making my monthly payments to the bank and paying my property and business taxes to the city, I am ahead of 4 years compare to the hard earner guy. I can still keep my job, just like him.

Then, after 4 years, what do you think will happen? My colleague will finally have earned enough to buy that same property, right? Well, there are strong chances that the property has gone up in value to reach, let say $250 000. Will he be working an extra year hoping that the value will not go any higher?

Even more ironic, when he can finally afford that property, from who is he buying from? From someone like me! I will be cashing the profit on his years of hard work. And sure, I will have to pay my fair share of tax on the profit made in real estate. Well, guess what?

Because I take the time to study the tax system, in most countries around the world, income taxes are calculated differently than capital gain, which is usually half taxed. So in other words, that $50 000 of profit, I am not paying $25 000 of taxes on it but $12 500 because it is capital gain.

This is just an example, please consult your tax expert when it comes to strategize your investments. What I what you to get in here is the mindset and where it leads. I reached my checkpoint and I found freedom and credit.

I leveraged y freedom and studied credit. I learnt different sets of rules, legal and official rules, that lead me to become a sophisticated investor. How many properties do you think that I bought? As many as the bank allowed me to buy!

And how do you think that I felt in the entire process? More and more powerful! That in turn fuelled my confidence to research and to do even more, bigger, bolder, faster!

Today, I am known more and more to be the **bridge** between the financial world and health professionals as I am anchoring the **Alphas** and helping companies to hit the stock market. It started with the first lesson of learning about credit and taxes!

So wherever you are, the time to start is now. Reach your checkpoint and be open to collect your reward. And sure, reward in this life is nothing more than the opportunity to be smarter and to work even harder, only now, you are keeping a bigger part of the upside.

We spent the whole chapter on the financial reward because that was the clear example that non can argue with. That upside is the minor part of the resources in reward if you compare it to the **boost in confidence and momentum** that you will be feeling.

Do it and react to your own body. Give yourself 5 years and write back to me. By then, I will surely be reading about you in a book or in the newspapers!

This is **TIMING, TIME MANAGEMENT ON STEROIDS** for Million Dollar Mindset. Welcome to the Alphas.

> "To solve time management in four single words: Get rid of procrastination."
> **Dr. BAK NGUYEN**

CHAPTER 6
"DISTRACTIONS"
by Dr. BAK NGUYEN

We are in chapter 6. If you've followed the logic of this journey and of my example, this is graduation. This means that after this chapter, you are ready to go and to leverage time yourself. Are you ready?

If we summarize our journey, we have identified the enemies: doubt and procrastination. We know where those 2 are coming from, the mind. We also know that the mind is slow. So the remedy to our enemies is **SPEED**.

And how can one gain speed? First, you have to start. Your best and only timing is always **NOW**. Only in movement can you gain speed. We also know that starting, you want to start with a **BANG** to ease your audience and or partners in, having them asking for more.

That, we are borrowing from the movie industry and their art of driving narrative. Don't laugh, it really works! After that **BANG**, you will have enough energy to start your next journey for about a quarter of the way.

By then, you will ways to keep your energy up. Jumping from one win to the next is your best bet as each win will empower you a little more. By now, your next win will be to pass the 50% mark of your journey. Writing books, that is easier to set but if you take the time to map your goals and project, you can map everything.

Mapping is not about defining the field, but your most precious resource, your time on that journey. Mapping, you will be creating the checkpoints as ladders. Only by mapping can you leverage **TIME**.

Now that you've started, that you have mapped, it's all about moving forward. Well, to grow within the process, you need to keep an open mind to react to your own actions and theirs consequences.

To start quickly, you can utilize templates, which are the mindset and tools from past experiences. Yours or others, that does not matter.

You can leverage the templates to move faster and not having to reinvent the wheel, but you still have to make that journey on your own. For that to happen, you must be open and flexible enough to diverge from your original plan.

Actually, this makes a lot of sense. If you keep your plan as is and that you made that plan at the beginning of your journey, what will you have learnt from that journey other than what you knew before starting that same journey?

So yes, you have to keep an open mind to react to your own actions and theirs consequences to make the journey your own. Moving quickly, you are assuring to have the best of your mind and it will set in **panic mode** and solve your problems instead of doubting and second-guessing each of your action.

And then, we learnt about the **GAMER MENTALITY**, about the use of checkpoints, and how to leverage those to collect your reward as you are moving ahead. This is more than enough for you to leverage **TIME** and to master the art of **TIMING**.

But before I graduate you and push you to try this mindset for yourself, there is another concept that I will like to share with you. How about **distractions**? On the way, you will find many of them, how can you stay on course? How do you keep focus?

First of all, how do you keep focus because we all know, even with the perfect timing, the best time management skills, you won't get anywhere unless you finish that journey. And that is your answer, focus on the finished line. That's my focus.

To keep me on track each day, I am looking for the immediate fun available. That can be jumping on the next win, connecting with new people, bounding with those sharing the journey with me. The idea is to do that while **accelerating** towards the finished line.

This may sound reversed to common sense but it really works. I've been there. In **MOMENTUM TRANSFER**, I shared the journey of how coach Dino Masson got me to resume physical training smoothly twice a week after 10 years or so, of interruption.

He asked me questions about business and entrepreneurship. That was not a diversion, he really wanted to know and understand more to support his own business. So I answered his questions just like I was on stage at a conference. By the time I finished my answer, I was through my training. And my trainings are physically intense!

We connected genuinely and he kept my mind busy answering while my body was following his coaching. That was a great way to reinitiate my training routine.

With the new connection made between business and physical training, I showed up twice a week for my sessions for years… until COVID. No complaints, no procrastination, no excuses. That's no distraction, it was fun and entertaining!

Then, I also tried the opposite. To write my books, I shared with you my routine already. But sometimes I am squeezed with a crazy timeframe having to write a book within a few days (just like this present challenge).

I tried to cut myself from everything and everyone to only emerge as I am done. Well, that is not working, at least not for me.

Cutting myself off from the world, I appreciated the silence for the first few hours. Unfortunately, writing a book takes more than a few hours. Then, I started to get bored. Because I isolated myself, I started to feel trapped. I respected my conditions and finished my isolation.

That book took much longer to finish. Worst, I did not enjoy the journey, but not at all. That title was **HYBRID**, which, until this day, is still left unedited. It was not a great experience, but now, I know.

To me, writing, and by extension, living is about connecting, discovering, and sharing. Each time I am sharing, the energy level goes up. As I am discovering new things, my excitement keeps the energy raising. And what to say about connecting?

Connect genuinely with another person and the energy available is not the sum of your energy, both energy will exponentially. That is what we called synergy.

Isolated and by myself, I wasn't looking for synergy, I was just looking for energy. The only person I had was the reflection in the mirror. That's not much synergy! This is when I understood that self-empowerment does not work!

So yes, I welcome the "**distractions**" for a lack of a better word. As I finish writing a book or even a chapter (checkpoint), sharing that with those I enjoy the company is a way to collect my reward. Sometimes, just enough to jump back in the next chapter.

Looking to grow more and more, at a faster rate and pace, I learnt to open up and not to judge anyone or anything. So no sorting, no preconceived ideas, no labels. I am open and very aware of how I feel. If the feeling is good, I keep going. If it feels wrong, I cut my losses and move on, quickly.

This has become my usual, hitting challenge and embarking on crazy challenges. Sure, I have my doubts and insecurities, like anyone, but the promise that I will meet new people, discover new things and maybe even find synergy, keeps my enthusiasm moving forward.

> "The fun part of the journey is
> what people call distraction."
> Dr. Bak Nguyen

That's quote #2496.

I am in it for the fun, so no I will never discount the distraction. My fun is also about sharing my journey and progress, so I can't afford to slow down for anyone, it will simply kill the fun!

This is a recipe that William, at 8, learnt to master and leverage. At 11, this is his 28th book as co-writer. He has given conferences, appeared in a multitude of videos and now, is hosting his own show. Well, we did all of that looking for fun and checkpoints.

> "A liability is an asset out of reach."
> Dr. Bak Nguyen

Talking about distractions, some will spin your head and through you off course. This will especially happen has there is sexual tension present. Well, energy is energy if you ask me. If the sexual tension was too much for you to bear, well, get stronger. Weren't we looking to grow, bigger, stronger, and wiser anyway?

And this is one of my great strengths as I embraced the **POWER OF YES**. Because I don't judge anyone nor anything, I see facts and possibilities. Then, I feel and acknowledge that feeling to empower. In the past, I was still looking to understand why. That's mind's stuff, full of doubts and excuses.

I feel and will try to be true to myself. That said, I am not sleeping with every pretty soul that I met. That is absolutely not what I meant. I meant to be open and available to connect.

> "As a genuine connecting happens, synergy will guide your actions, synergy, not lust nor desire."
> Dr. Bak Nguyen

That's quote #2497.

Energy is what we are and what we are looking for. Energy, just like gravity will pull you in. On that, you will be attracted by energy with your reverse polarity, that's a law of physic. That's the attraction part.

If you are empowering that connection and are getting closer and closer, the tension will rise exponentially until fusion. This is where even more energy gets released, often in a blast. Are you ready to experience that blast or even, explosion?

Keep in mind that each of these explosions might through you off course. That's the risk, that's the fun. As for me, as I am choosing my battles, I am also choosing my explosions. I have my goals, those I am not changing. What I am very open about is how and how fast I will get to these goals.

I don't mind changing my checkpoints, for as long as it will either be a shortcut (being faster) or one releasing great energy, which will accelerate my race. In both cases, I am accelerating.

Those distractions I haven't taken, I have to face the truth, it was because I wasn't strong enough. I wasn't ready for these explosions. This is when that connection becomes a liability, a distraction. I was the problem because I was not ready. The labelling is not on them, it is on me. And those will come with a price.

We are talking about real and genuine connections here, not casual encounters. That said, most explosions are messy and will disrupt your present equilibrium. Be ready to face the consequences of your choices and actions.

That said, once you are ready, don't stand there, trying to keep things as is. By doing so, you are trying to absorb the energy of the blast instead of being empowered by it. It will burn you alive.

And even if you survive the blast and the healing, you have become stronger surviving, you haven't learnt anything about surfing and leveraging empowerment!

This is **TIMING, TIME MANAGEMENT ON STEROIDS** for Million Dollar Mindset. Welcome to the Alphas.

"To solve time management in four single words: Get rid of procrastination."

Dr. BAK NGUYEN

CHAPTER 7
"SYNERGY"
by Dr. BAK NGUYEN

I know that I left you hanging on a cliffhanger finishing the last chapter. Well, haven't taught you to have your audience asking for more?

You have now graduated, have you noticed? If you are wondering about distractions, checkpoints, and synergy, you are projecting yourself forward and you are already feeling the excitement or anxiety in your belly. Either way, this is great, because you feel, you know that this is real!

Now back at the explosions and synergy. No, I won't be sharing with you that story. Instead, I will be sharing with you an even better one, the Cinderella fairy tale that I shared with William.

I was in the midst of my midlife crisis and facing some crucial choices about my future. The tension and traction were through the roof and everyone could feel the imminent explosion coming soon.

I can only canalized as much energy as I could harness to propel me further on my quest writing 15 books within 15 months. But I must admit that the tension and traction were more powerful than me. I kept pulling. I was exhausted. I barely finished my challenge, writing my 15th book and setting that new world record.

At the checkpoint, I was expecting the reward, synergy, sex! Well, it came in in a much different form. William, 8 at that time, set in and asked about when are we going to write our first book together. That was such a surprise.

Suddenly, what I felt was not the traction nor the tension anymore, it was serenity, silence, and the freshness of the horizon. That's what I felt. And it felt good.

My mind was trying to process the information. It got stuck on keeping my word to my son. That was the official narrative. What really happened is the explosion from the tension and traction that never happened. Instead, it got me to implode. With the energy released, William surfed and fused, creating a new synergy.

This is how History will say that to celebrate a world record, we scored 2 new ones, within a month! And then, from the new synergy and from the energy at each checkpoint, we broke the sound barrier, going from **15 books written within 15 months** to **36 books written within 18 months + 1 week**! And this is my story.

Was William a distraction? Sure! Was William the best synergy I ever experienced? Of course! It is always easy to label the past and to make sense of our decisions and justify our choices afterward.

Even if William saved my marriage, I did what I felt strongly about, I followed the energy trail. That is why that story has a happy ending, the story of tension and midlife crisis.

But much greater than the ending was the beginning and the rise of Dr. Bak and William Bak together, as father and son, as buddies.

This journey, writing **TIMING**, I am leveraging on the synergy and the bounding that William and I found almost 3 years ago. Just like in space, the aftershock and the wavelength of an explosion can be felt from a great distance, both in space and time.

That was the **BANG** that started our legend together. We surfed on that wave for almost 2 years. As the momentum is stable, William and I are looking for our next checkpoint to renew our synergy.

This is also why, the next chapter of this journey, you will be reading from him, to have his version of the story, his feelings, and his perspectives.

Today, William is a pre-teenager and you can feel his hormones emerging. He is experiencing a burst of sexual hormones as his own body is changing. I am a strong presence at his side but because we shared that synergy together, he does not stand in my shadow. Instead, we empower one another.

Was that good **TIMING** on William's part? In this story and narrative, the answer is absolute. In truth, he felt an explosion coming and offered an alternative, the promise of a father to his son. Then, he went all-in, fulfilling that promise and living the legend that we were writing.

I was doing the same, reacting to the energy and feelings much more than thinking. I won't fool myself nor fool you saying that this was wisdom and an informed decision. I did not think, I felt, and went with what I felt strongly. I did not say what felt right, but what I felt the strongest. And that will be your truth!

> "Feelings don't lie. Since there are many truths, yours lays in the strongest of your feelings."
> Dr. Bak Nguyen

That's quote #2498.

Because it was my strongest feeling, I had a chance to leverage it and to make a great narrative out of it. I am still talking in books' wording but actually, it is my life that I am sharing with you. Because the feeling was strong, I know that it was genuine. And thanks to that, the explosion was constructive instead of devastating.

How about that for a journey? I know, the subjects of this book were **TIMING** and **TIME MANAGEMENT**. I changed the rules as I replaced **MANAGEMENT** with **LEVERAGE**.

And this is why I am sharing with you this story, because, with leverage, they are consequences. Understand them well, know the mapping and you will be collecting your rewards at each checkpoint.

Overthinking and being stuck with your doubts, you will miss on all the checkpoints and theirs rewards. To have access to those, you need to be available and to feel without filters.

I thought that I reached the end of the line with that record of **15 books within 15 months**. Fortunately, I was open and welcomed the distraction and the possibilities. I was open and available to face the consequences of my actions and decisions. This is how I collected my reward. And then, I surfed!

About **TIMING** and **TIME MANAGEMENT**, I did more within the last 4 years than in my first 40. The timing is **NOW** and forget about management. Be open and available and then, be genuine. Start with yourself, acknowledge what you feel, without filter, without excuses.

Then, empower these feelings, they are the strongest of what you are, vibrating and resonating in the universe. Just like music, the more space you have, the stronger will be the sound. The more open and available you are, the stronger and powerful will be your emotions, your frequency.

I started my journey writing books in my own Quest of Identity. Well, my Identity is my frequency. It has grown since, from confidence and training, but mainly thanks to synergy and momentum.

Actually, the momentum did not grow my frequency, it just pushed it further and faster so I have more chance to find synergy. What is next, what is more, I am eager to see! I am available.

As for William, my dear son, your first great journey have started with a big **BANG**. You have not only survived that explosion, you grew from it. You learnt to surf the wave and to leverage **SYNERGY**. I am so grateful to share their rise with you.

I won't have to teach you, all I need to do is to keep sharing with you. In other words, I do not have to stop my rise to be with you, you are a big part of my rise as I am the beginning of yours. William, thank you! How about that for efficiency and time management?

We have the tendency to compartmentalize everything, building walls everywhere. Well, we are wasting much time and resources lying to ourselves since no life with emerge from there. Life is dynamic, Life is synergy. In other words, Life is messy, until you understood its vibe and merge within.

In common language, we are talking about finding our voice. There is much truth in that. The real wording was to release your frequency. Not to find but to release since we all know who we are deep down. It is what we feel. We just need to turn down the security protection and open the gate.

For that, you need to fool your mind, at least to jumpstart your process. Then, don't put it back in control but don't discard it either, it is your best engineer, your best lieutenant. That's the release.

Now about **frequency**, you are not your words, your thoughts, your voice. You are generating all of those. You are what you feel at the dawn of the day before your mind awakes. You are what you see late at night when your mind is tired and has checked out. That's you! The real you.

If you think that you are your mind, what happens every time that your mind checks out? Is your heart checking out for a pause? Now you know your own hierarchy of what is you and what should be in power. And your heart, captain of the ship, has access to all of your body, emotions, hormones to stir your ship.

It does not have to command or convinced, it just beat to empower the rest of your body, including the brain. Now, you feel the power! Now, you've touched the power of truth, the power of you! That's your frequency!

From here, each of your journeys will push you forward to look for energy, for fun. On your way, you will find distractions, many of them. Be kind, be open, those are possibilities. When you are ready, one of them might become your way, your big break!

Haven't I told you to keep moving and more resources lay ahead? Those are the distractions on your path. Be strong enough and you will leverage those within reach. Be careful not to overextend yourself. You still have your current journey to focus on.

Be open, be available but don't be greedy. If you are fully aware of your feelings and emotions, you will feel what is right for you and what to do. On that, the first feeling is the right one, before your mind has the time to catch up.

It might seem that I have something against the mind. Well, yes and no. You know that my intelligence is my most powerful attribute, I don't think that I still have to prove myself anymore. And yet, intelligence alone brought much more misery than victories.

> "The day that I set my intelligence at the service of my feelings, that day, I became powerful, vibrating in synergy with the Universe."
> **Dr. Bak Nguyen**

That's quote #2499.

That's not bragging, that's acknowledgement. And this is how twisted our minds can be. So I love my logic and intelligence, not as a captain but a lieutenant, a servant, one not in command.

The other reason that I will never leave control ever again to my mind is that the mind is what Conformity, religion, culture, education, and society access to control my behaviour. Now, I know what they expect and will not go to war. I will simply stop taking that as the one and only truth anymore.

Just like me, you too are looking for your rise. It does not have to be messy, forced, nor to explode. Those are the results of keeping a force of nature (because yes, you are a force of nature, we all are) caged for too long. Once you've free that force, feel it to understand it and it will empower you to rise.

Ride your emotions and you are in for a great journey. If you stop trying to control your emotions, you will feel their power and leverage them in your favour. That is to find yourself, your frequency.

To find synergy, be open to the frequency of others. This is what William did as he offered himself to stabilize me as

I was imploding. Instead of trying to control the energy, we released it and surfed the waves together.

Now you know enough, it is time for you to try, to feel. That's the only way forward, to feel and to try. Knowing is much overrated, it won't lead you where you want to go!

Your timing is **NOW** and your key is to **try** and To **feel**. Then, empower your emotions to find your truth, your reality. As you feel, you know what you are, you won't need motivation and management anymore! Those were to appeal to your mind as you are in a hybrid phase.

Feeling, you know what you like and dislike. Feeling you know what is right, even if you have never tasted it before! Try and adapt, that's growth. You are now free. You are powerful. Go to your powers and to your happiness!

This is **TIMING, TIME MANAGEMENT ON STEROIDS** for Million Dollar Mindset. Welcome to the Alphas.

"To solve time management in four single words: Get rid of procrastination."

Dr. BAK NGUYEN

CHAPTER 8
"ON STEROIDS"
by WILLIAM BAK

Now, it's my time to talk. After 2 hours of listening to my dad, Dr. Bak, I needed that. I know that Dr. Bak is smart and all but I can stand listening for too long without talking. This is my chapter, so yes, I will talk. Now, I still need to have something smart to say! For as long as it might be fun, why not.

I would like to start with the fact that my father is not pushing me, I am pushing him! I pushed him to write books with me. I made videos and even went on stage to say that. I am very proud to say that I have pushed Dr. Bak to write books, more books.

And that is what I was looking for, more! I wanted to spend more time with my father, more and more time. Then, we shared a connection. I was not even sure what a connection was by then. And without preparation and warning, the word appeared in my mouth as we were making videos to talk about the writing of our books, the chicken books. You can find them on my Instagram account, look for William Bak.

"I will show you, I won't force you but I won't wait for you."
William Bak & Dr. Bak Nguyen

That's our first quote together. Well, I guess, it is my first quote ever. I love it. It is so true. Since that day, this is really my relationship with my father. I trust him and I love him. He does not push me, he shows me stuff and then, he moved on. If I want to spend time with him, it is now for me to run.

That's how we wrote books together. We are also taking this to the pool. Before, he was swimming laps faster than me. Today, he is not a challenge for me anymore. I just like to do 2, 4, or even 6 laps more than him. I love to beat my dad! We have fun, we do not wait for one another, and yet, we are often together.

Since we shared that special connection, we are spending a lot of time together. I love him for that. Actually, I love my life! Writing books? Not so much anymore. I love playing video games and playing with my toys, Transformers.

Well, my dad used that too! I guess the word he will be using is leverage! I was much younger as I travelled with my mom and him to the USA to visit and buy houses, a lot of houses. I was bored, those houses were not really big or did not have pools and stuff.

It was just boring. Then my father told me that for each house visited, if I behave, I will have a toy! Since that day, I love visiting houses. Papa, can we see more?

Then it was in the pool. Younger, I liked to hang around in the pool and play with my toys, in the water. My dad, he just swims laps and as he is done, goes back in the house.

To encourage me to swim, he told me that he will buy me Transformers for the laps I will swim that day. I did 80 laps the first time. Eventually, I reached 100 laps once!

I know that my dad is a man of his words, so I swam. Eventually, it became easy. I did not want to stop. I had many, many transformers by now. I spent so much of his money on those… sorry papa!

Today, I am a very good swimmer. I may not be ready for the Olympics but I can easily beat my dad in the pool! And never, he has forced me. He invited me and if I want my reward, I better beat him at his own game!

Now, I do not swim for Transformers anymore. I swim to beat him and to have video games time. I am not a kid anymore, video games are now my favourite. Even then, he managed to make a game out of it.

In COVID times, I got addicted to a game called FORTNITE. Playing that game, I lost some of the connections I shared with my dad. I felt bad. He helped me. Not just by cutting my video games times (on that, yes, I got cut but I needed that break).

Then he offered me to play video games in front of a camera. He was having many interviews on camera talking to **ALPHAS** from all around the world. I wanted to be an **ALPHA** too but not talking about serious stuff. Playing video games, that works with me!

We created **GAMEBAK**, my own show to review mobile games. That was last year. I enjoy that time in front of the camera because I spent time with my dad. I felt that we were having back that great connection.

Then, one day, we passed in front of an EB GAMES shop and my dad asked if there had PlayStation 5 consoles in store. The saleswoman said yes and we bought it! I couldn't believe it. My dad bought me a PS5! Don't get me wrong, I love my PS4 at home, but a PS5!!!

Then, we pushed **GAMEBAK** to the next level, reviewing now games from PS4 and PS5. As my dad has his challenge of writing 100 books, me too, I have my challenge: I will cover each of the 850 + games available on PS Now, the streaming service. PS Now is kind of a Netflix but for games.

Once again, my dad is not forcing me. We encourage each other. From Transformers to video games, he knows what I love and he buys a lot of them for me. Me, not to be spoiled as the kid in *Harry Potter*, I need to earn them, each of them. And this is why our connection is so special.

I learnt to write books! By the way, at the beginning, I just need to speak and he was writing for me. Then, he made me write a book on paper! I hated that! We even stopped writing books for a while after that one. Then, lately, we had a deal, I will write by myself but like him, from a computer. That, I like.

I wrote the French version of our last chicken book by myself, **CHICKEN FOREVER**. Today, I write articles, always in French because my French is not as good… and that I need to go to Jean-Eudes, the private high school where my dad went.

Well, I am covering some of the 850 + games writing about them. You can read my reviews on Medium.com, look for William Bak! Of course, my dad is helping me with the correction of my texts. Hey, I am still a kid and I am 11!

So I learnt to write books and articles, both in English and French. I learnt to swim, pretty fast. I also learnt to be in front of a camera talking. Talking, that I like. Today, I have my own show and I am also becoming the youngest host of the **ALPHASHOW**, my dad's show for a special series called **COVIDCONOMICS**.

For that, we travelled all across Canada to shoot videos. I love travelling! I know that I will have to learn to edit videos soon. I am not sure of that one.

Today, my dad, **the Dr. Bak**, is asking for my help. I said yes! I always say YES to my dad. Well, that's not true, but if I want him to say YES to my requests for favours (video games), I have to say YES to him first.

Well, he needed my help to ask him questions for his next book, **TIMING**. All I had to do was to be on camera with him asking questions. I was okay with that! Talking is easy for me. Helping my dad, I will always be ready. And if he is happy, it will be pretty easy for me to ask for favours.

Little did I know what will be coming next. The beginning was long and boring as my dad was answering the questions with smart and long answers. It became fun as I could talk, and I did! Then after close to 2 hours of interview, we had so much fun together than he decided to put my name on the book too!

I was afraid that I need to write my chapters but this is the **APOLLO protocol**, we just need to talk, to say smart stuff, and the computer and my dad will take care of the writing.

Now I am back at the beginning, of what I loved when all I need was to talk and my dad was writing for me! As I will be reading this chapter, a few days later, I realized that my dad made a lot, a lot of corrections. But it is all true, this is our story together! I love you papa!

So, to make it into the book, I have to answer the questions too. To the question of **TOOLS OF PRODUCTIVITY**, my answer made both of us laugh: you (my dad)! He his my greatest tool, if I can use that word. He knows how to write from his iPhone (with 2 thumbs up) and his laptop. He knows how to make and edit videos. Me, I know him!

I still need to do my part. I give ideas and when it is my turn, I am talking in front of the camera. That's easy. Then,

I learnt to write by myself and to swim faster than him. Do you know that I have special eyes for taking great pictures too? Lately, I am his photographer, and sometimes, I direct behind the camera too. I guess editing will not be that hard to learn after all!

I don't know much about **TIMING** and **MANAGEMENT**. To most of the other questions on focus, Stress, of what when I do facing boring stuff, well my answer is pretty short. I look for fun. When it is fun, there is no stress and nothing is boring. Focus… what is that again?

I have fun with my dad. I have fun and we know that thanks to our books and our shows, we are inspiring many people. This is even more fun! It is super cool. It is awesome if you ask me! For that, I love my dad, **the Dr. Bak**!

What else do you want to know? Don't ask me too many questions, I am still a kid and it's been more than 2 hours already! Can we take a break?

If there is something that I learnt from my dad is that it is always possible, there is always a way for more, more, and much more! We just need to find that way. For as long as it is fun, I want it **NOW**! When can we start? That is what I know about **TIMING**.

Oh, and one last thing. I was about to forget. Something else that my father taught me was to open my mind. We wrote about that in the chicken books, to open your mind and to open your heart. Well, lately, we loved to watch Hell's Kitchen with chef Gordon Ramsay.

Well, that gave me the opportunity to open my mind. Since Hell's Kitchen, I am much more open to try new food! I even learnt new words like risotto and raw! My dad is not a chef but he was the first person who taught me to be open-minded.

I watch my dad working hard and writing his books. He is up early in the morning. Me, I am still sleeping by then, but I believe him. Every morning when I woke up, he is already finishing his chapter! I like to celebrate with him, especially when he finished a book!

He wrote 2 million words or almost. I cannot write as much. I write 300 words for each of my articles. How many do I have until now? I think 10 or so? That's, wait a minute… 3000 words! Wow, that's a lot of words that I wrote!

We are buddy-buddy, my dad and I. Just like swimming, I will beat him writing books one day… I may not write, I love the **APPOLO protocol** thing!

I am already cooler than him, maybe not as smart, but way cooler than him on camera and I am still young! I am just 11 years old! I will beat him one day and we will celebrate together, my dad and I!

I am William Bak, C-O-O-L, cool, I salute you. Welcome to the Alphas.

This is **TIMING, TIME MANAGEMENT ON STEROIDS** for Million Dollar Mindset. Welcome to the Alphas.

Dr. BAK NGUYEN

CONCLUSION
by Dr. BAK NGUYEN

That was William, my evolution on **STEROIDS**. Well, let stop for a minute and see the big picture here: we are talking about **TIME MANAGEMENT**, in other words, of increasing efficiency and outcome.

Well, William just helped me to write my next book within 3 hours as he learnt about the **APOLLO protocol** while entertaining you. For his openness and effort, he also earned his name on the cover of this book, **TIMING, TIME MANAGEMENT ON STEROIDS**.

More than the confidence and the time spent as father and son, William is making the most of his summer vacation days. How about that as **MANAGEMENT** style?

The answer to **TIMING** is **NOW**, always. The key to avoid management is **FUN**, that you heard from William pretty clearly.

> "Have fun and many of the questions simply fade away."
> Wiliam Bak

But if you must know, to manage and to leverage, you need a map. Learning from my writing experience, we learnt to map the journey ahead, not in a rigid way that will leave us only with what we knew before we began. We map our most precious resource, **TIME** while we are open on the alternatives and on how to get to the finished line.

From the beginning of this journey, the enemies were very well-identified: **DOUBTS** and **PROCRASTINATION** (excuses). These two, we know where they lay, in the mind. We also know that the mind is a slow runner and will always be playing catch-up. So **SPEED** became our remedy.

And **SPEED**, how do you generate that? Moving from win to win is a great way to keep the energy up and to build momentum. Utilizing the templates is a great way to ease your way in with speed and to react to your own results.

Only by reacting you will slowly uncover and release your frequency, your voice. And this is where your legend will begin.

We learnt, from the technic of writing books, to start with a **BANG** to ease your audience in and to set the pace. Then, we learnt to surf that energy for as long as possible without stretching it artificially. This is where we learnt about the checkpoints and the rewards, the **GAMING MENTALITY**.

From the rewards, I showed you how to harness your power, riding your emotions to new heights. This should be enough! But then, one last thing, we learnt about **DISTRACTION** which will ease and fuelled your journey with **FUN** and possibilities.

And from **DISTRACTION**, we discovered, together, **SYNERGY**. This is no theory but a testimony. To close the journey, you heard from William and his side of **the story of SYNERGY**. Yes, this whole journey is about believing, to believe and to feel. Actually, it is simpler than that:

> "Feel to believe."
> Dr. Bak Nguyen

That's quote #2500.

Your **TIMING** is **NOW**, always. This has been a magical journey. With William and the **APPOLO protocol**, I have successfully resumed my Momentum writing. In less than an hour, I will be joining Jonas for an interview and I will have reached my goal, to finish this book, **TIMING, TIME**

MANAGEMENT ON STEROIDS before going on the show. 2 days of writing and maybe 6 more hours of correction and editing.

From the bottom of my heart, I thank William for his help and empowerment. With this book completed, I still have 4 books to write and 20 days to go. That's 5 days per book! William and the **APOLLO protocol** just raise my odds up by much, 14.4 hours per book! This is more than I could hope for.

I am amazed and very hopeful about the future, about my future, about William's, and about yours. Open your heart and listen to your feelings. Then, go to your powers. You now know the way and the how!

This is the shortest of all of my conclusion. Well, keep it short and sweet, time is of the essence!

This is **TIMING, TIME MANAGEMENT ON STEROIDS** for Million Dollar Mindset. Welcome to the Alphas.

Dr. BAK NGUYEN

ANNEX
GLOSSARY OF Dr. BAK's LIBRARY

1

1SELF -080

REINVENT YOURSELF FROM ANY CRISIS
BY Dr. BAK NGUYEN

In 1SELF is about to reinvent yourself to rise from any crisis. Written in the midst of the COVID war, now more than ever, we need hope and the know-how to bridge the future. More than just the journey of Dr. Bak, this time, Dr. Bak is sharing his journey with mentors and people who built part of the world as we know it. Interviewed in this book, CHRISTIAN TRUDEAU, former CEO and FOUNDER of BCE EMERGIS (BELL CANADA), he also digitalized the Montreal Stock Exchange. RON KLEIN, American Innovator, inventor of the magnetic stripe of the credit card, of MLS (Multi-listing services) and the man who digitalized WALL STREET bonds markets. ANDRE CHATELAIN, former first vice-president of the MOVEMENT DES JARDINS. Dr. JEAN DE SERRES, former CEO of HEMA QUEBEC. These men created billions in values and have changed our lives, even without us knowing. They all come together to share their experiences and knowledge to empower each and everyone to emerge stronger from this crisis, from any crisis.

AFTERMATH -063
BUSINESS AFTER THE GREAT PAUSE
BY Dr. BAK NGUYEN & Dr. ERIC LACOSTE

In AFTERMATH, Dr. Bak joins forces with Community leader and philanthrope Dr. Eric Lacoste. Two powerful minds and forces of nature in the reaction to the worst economic meltdown in modern times. We are all victims of the CORONA virus. Both just like humans have learned to adapt to survive, so is our economy. Most business structures and management philosophies are inherited from the age of industrialization and beyond. COVID-19 has shot down the world economy with months. At the time of the AFTERMATH, the truth is many corporations and organizations will either have to upgrade to the INFORMATION AGE or disappear. More than the INFORMATION upgrade, the era of SOCIAL MEDIA and the MILLENNIALS are driving a revolution in the core philosophy of all organizations. Profit is not king anymore, support is. In this time and age where a teenager with a social account can compete with the million dollars PR firm, social implication is now the new cornerstone. Those who will adapt will prevail and prosper, while the resistance and old guards will soon be forgotten as fossils of a past era.

ALPHA LADDERS -075
CAPTAIN OF YOUR DESTINY
BY Dr. BAK NGUYEN & JONAS DIOP

In ALPHA LADDERS, Dr. Bak is sharing his private conversation and board meetings with 2 of his trusted lieutenants, strategist Jonas Diop and international Counsellor, Brenda Garcia. As both the Dr. Bak and ALPHA brands are gaining in popularity and traction, it was time to get the movement to the next level. Now, it's about building a community and to help everyone willing to become ALPHAS to find their powers. Dr. Bak is a natural recruiter of ALPHAS and peers. He also spent the last 20 years plus, training and mentoring proteges. Now comes the time to empower more and more proteges to become ALPHAS. ALPHAS LADDERS is the journey of how Dr. Bak went from a product of Conformity to rise into a force of Nature, know as a kind tornado. In ALPHA LADDERS Jonas pushed Dr. Bak to retrace each of the steps of his awakening, steps that we can breakdown and reproduce for ourselves. The goal is to empower each willing individual to become the ultimate Captain of his or her destiny, and to do it, again and again. Welcome to the Alphas.

ALPHA LADDERS 2 -081
SHAPING LEADERS AND ACHIEVERS
BY Dr. BAK NGUYEN & BRENDA GARCIA

In ALPHA LADDERS 2, Dr. Bak is sharing the second part of his private conversation and board meetings with his trusted lieutenants. This time it is with international Counsellor, Brenda Garcia that the dialogue is taking place. In this second tome, the journey is taken to the next level. If the first tome was about the WHYs and the HOWs at an individual level, this tome is about the WHYs and the HOWs at the societal level. Through the lens of her background in international relations and diplomacy, Brenda now has the mission to help Dr. Bak establish structures, not only for his emerging organization and legacy, THE ALPHAS, but to also inspire all the other leaders and structures of our society. To do this, Brenda is taking Dr. Bak on an anthropological, sociological and philosophical journey to revisit different historical key moments in various fields and eras, going as far back as in ancient Greece at the dawn of democracy, all the way to the golden era of modern multilateralism embodied by the UN structure. Learning from the legacies of prominent figures going from Plato to Ban Ki Moon, Martin Luther King or Nelson Mandela, to Machiavelli, Marx and Simone de Beauvoir, Brenda and Dr. Bak are attempting to grasp the essence of structure and hierarchy, their goal being to empower each willing individual to become the ultimate Captain of their own success, to climb up the ladders no matter how high it is, and to build their legacy one step at a time.

AMONGST THE ALPHAS -058
BY Dr. BAK NGUYEN, with Dr. MARIA KUNDSTATER, Dr. PAUL OUELLETTE and Dr. JEREMY KRELL

In AMONGST THE ALPHAS Dr. Bak opens the blueprint of the next level with the hope that everyone can be better, bigger, wiser, but above all, a philosophy of Life that if, well applied, can bring inspiration to life. The Alphas rose in the midst of the COVID war as an International Collaboration to empower individuals to rise from the global crisis. Joining Dr. Bak are some of the world thinkers and achievers, the Alphas. Doctors, business people, thinkers, achievers, influencers, they are coming together to define what is an Alpha and his or her role, making the world a better place. This isn't the American dream, it is the human dream, one that can help you make History. Joining Dr. Bak are 3 Alpha authors, Dr. Maria Kundstater, Dr. Paul Ouellette and Dr. Jeremy Krell. This book started with questions from coach Jonas Diop. Welcome to the Alphas.

AMONGST THE ALPHAS vol.2 -059
ON THE OTHER SIDE
BY Dr. BAK NGUYEN with Dr. JULIO REYNAFARJE, Dr. LINA DUSEVICIUTE and Dr. DUC-MINH LAM-DO

In AMONGST THE ALPHAS 2, Dr. Bak continues to explore the meaning of what it is to be an Alpha and how to act amongst Alphas, because as the saying taught us: alone one goes fast, together we goes far. Some people see the problem. Some people look at the problem, some people created the problem. Some people leverage the problem into solutions and opportunities. Well, all of those people are Alphas. Networking and leveraging one another, their powers and reach are beyond measure. And one will keep the other in line too. Joining Dr. Bak are 3 Alphas from around the world coming together to share and collaborate, Dr. DUSEVICIUTE, Dr. LAM-DO and Dr. REYNAFARJE. This isn't the American dream, it is the human dream, one that can help you make History. Welcome to the Alphas.

BOOTCAMP -071
BOOKS TO REWRITE MINDSETS INTO WINNING STATES OF MIND
BY Dr. BAK NGUYEN

In BOOTCAMP 8 BOOKS TO REWRITE MINDSETS INTO WINNING STATES OF MIND, Dr. Bak is taking you into his past, before the visionary entrepreneur, before the world records, before the Industry's disruptor status. Here are 8 of the books that changed Dr. Bak's thinking and, therefore, reset his evolution into the course we now know him for. BOOTCAMP: 8 BOOKS TO REWRITE MINDSETS INTO WINNING STATES OF MIND, is a Bootcamp of 8 weeks for anyone looking to experience Dr. Bak's training to become THE Dr. BAK you came to know and love. This book will summarize how each title changed Dr. Bak mindset into a state of mind and how he applied that to rewrite his destiny. 8 books to read, that's 8 weeks of Bootcamp to access the power of your MIND and of your WILL. Are you ready for a change?

BRANDING -044
BALANCING STRATEGY AND EMOTIONS
BY Dr. BAK NGUYEN

BRANDING is communication to its most powerful state. Branding is not just about communicating anymore but about making a promise, about establishing a relation, about generating an emotion. More than once, Dr. Bak proved himself to be a master, communicating and branding his ideas into flags attracting interest and influences, nationally and internationally. In BRANDING, Dr. Bak shares a very unique and personal journey, branding Dr. Bak. How does he go from Dr. Nguyen, a loved and respected dentist to becoming Dr. Bak, a world anchor hosting THE ALPHAS in the medical and financial world?More than a personal journey, BRANDING helps to break down the steps to elevate someone with nothing else but the force of his or her spirit. Welcome to the Alphas.

CHANGING THE WORLD FROM A DENTAL CHAIR -007
BY Dr. BAK NGUYEN

Since he has received the EY's nomination for entrepreneur of the year for his startup Mdex & Co, Dr. Bak Nguyen has pushed the opportunity to the next level. Speaker, author, and businessman, Dr. Bak is a true entrepreneur and industries' disruptor. To compensate for the startup's status of Mdex & Co, he challenged himself to write a book based on the EY's questionnaire to share an in-depth vision of his company. With "Changing the World from a dental chair" Dr. Bak is sharing his thought process and philosophy to his approach to the industry. Not looking to revolutionize but rather to empower, he became, despite himself, an industries disruptor: an entrepreneur who has established a new benchmark. Dr. Bak Nguyen is a cosmetic dentist and visionary businessman who won the GRAND HOMAGE prize of "LYS de la Diversité" 2016, for his contribution as a citizen and entrepreneur in the community. He also holds recognitions from the Canadian Parliament and the Canadian Senate.

In 2003, he founded Mdex, a dental company upon which in 2018, he launched the most ambitious private endeavour to reform the dental industry, Canada wide. He wrote seven books covering ENTREPRENEURSHIP, LEADERSHIP, QUEST of IDENTITY, and now, PROFESSION HEALTH. Philosopher, he has close to his heart the quest of happiness of the people surrounding him, patients, and colleagues alike. Those projects have allowed Dr. Nguyen to attract interests from the international and diplomatic community and he is now the centre of a global discussion on the wellbeing and the future of the health profession. It is in that matter that he shares with you his thoughts and encourages the health community to share their own stories.

CHAMPION MINDSET -039
LEARNING TO WIN
BY Dr. BAK NGUYEN & CHRISTOPHE MULUMBA

CHAMPION MINDSET is the encounter of the business world and the professional sports world. Industries' Disruptor Dr. BAK NGUYEN shares his wisdom and views with the HAMMER, CFL Football Star, Edmonton's Eskimos CHRISTOPHE MULUMBA on how to leverage on the champion mindset to create successful entrepreneurs. Writing and challenging each other, they discovered the parallels and the difference of both worlds, but mainly, the recipe for leveraging from one to succeed in the other, from champions and entrepreneurs to WINNERS. Build and score your millions, it is a matter of mindset! This is CHAMPION MINDSET.

EMPOWERMENT -069
BY Dr. BAK NGUYEN

In EMPOWERMENT, Dr. Bak's 69th book, writing a book every 8 days for 8 weeks in a row to write the next world record of writing 72 books/36 months, Dr. Bak is taking a rest, sharing his inner feelings, inspiration, and motivation. Much more than his dairy, EMPOWERMENT is the key to walk in his footsteps and to comprehend the process of an overachiever. Dr. Bak's helped and inspired countless people to find their voice, to live their dream, and to be the better version of themselves. Why is he sharing as much and keep sharing? Why is he going that fast, always further and further, why and how is he keeping his inspiration and momentum? Those are all the answers EMPOWERMENT will deliver to you. This book might be one of the fastest Dr. Bak has written, not because of time constraints but from inspiration, pure inspiration to share and to grow. There is always a dark side to each power, two faces to a coin. Well, this is the less prominent facets of Dr. Bak Momentum and success, the road to his MINDSET.

FORCES OF NATURE -015
FORGING THE CHARACTER OF WINNERS
BY Dr. BAK NGUYEN

In FORCES OF NATURE, Dr. Bak is giving his all. This is his 15 books written within 15 months. It is the end of a marathon to set the next world record. For the occasion, he wanted to end with a big bang! How about a book with all of his biggest challenges? A Quest of Identity, a journey looking for his name and powers, Dr. Bak is borrowing with myths and legends to make this journey universal. Yes, this is Dr. Bak's mythology. Demons, heroes and Gods, there are forces of Nature that we all meet on our way for our name. Some will scare us, some will fight us, some will manipulate us. We can flee, we can hide, we can fight. What we do will define our next encounter and the one after. A tale of personal growth, a journey to find power and purpose, Dr. Bak is showing us the path to freedom, the Path of Life. Welcome to the Alphas.

HORIZON, BUILDING UP THE VISION -045
VOLUME ONE
BY Dr. BAK NGUYEN

Dr. Bak is opening up at your demand! Many of you are following Dr. Bak online and are asking to know more about his lifestyle. This is how he has chosen to respond: sharing his lifestyle as he traveled the world and what he learned in each city to come to build his Mindset as a driver and a winner. Here are 10 destinations (over 69 that will be following in the next volumes...) in which he shares his journey. New York, Quebec, Paris, Punta Cana, Monaco, Los Angeles, Nice, Holguin, the journey happened over twenty years.

HORIZON, ON THE FOOTSTEP OF TITANS -048
VOLUME TWO
BY Dr. BAK NGUYEN

Dr. Bak is opening up at your demand! Many of you are following Dr. Bak online and are asking to know more about his lifestyle. This is how he has chosen to respond: sharing his lifestyle as he traveled the world and what he learned in each city to come to build his Mindset as a driver and a winner. Here are 9 destinations (over 72 that will be following in the next volumes...) in which he shares his journey. Hong Kong, London, Rome, San Francisco, Anaheim, and more..., the journey happened over twenty years. Dr. Bak is sharing with you his feelings, impressions, and how they shaped his state of mind and character into Dr. Bak. From a dreamer to a driver and a builder, the journey started since he was 3. Wealth is a state of mind, and a state of mind is the basis of the drive. Find out about the mind of an Industry's disruptor.

HORIZON, Dr.EAMING OF THE FUTURE -068
VOLUME THREE
BY Dr. BAK NGUYEN

Dr. Bak is back. From the midst of confinement, he remembers and writes about what life was, when traveling was a natural part of Life. It will come back. Now more than ever, we need to open both our hearts and minds to fight fear and intolerance. Writing from a time of crisis, he is sharing the magic and psychological effect of seeing the world and how it has shaped his mindset. Here are 9 other destinations (over 75) in which he shares his journey. Beijing, Key West, Madrid, Amsterdam, Marrakech and more..., the journey happened over twenty years.

HOW TO NOT FAIL AS A DENTIST -047
BY Dr. BAK NGUYEN

In HOW TO NOT FAIL AS A DENTIST, Dr. Bak is given 20 plus years of experience and knowledge of what it is to be a dentist on the ground. PROFESSIONAL INTELLIGENCE, FINANCIAL INTELLIGENCE and MANAGEMENT INTELLIGENCE are the fields that any dentist will have to master for a chance to success and a shot for happiness practicing dentistry. Where ever you are starting your career as a new graduate or a veteran in the field looking to reach the next level, this is book smart and street smart all into one. This is Million Dollar Mindset applied to dentistry. We won't be making a millionaire out of you from this book, we will be giving you a shot to happiness and success. The million will follow soon enough.

HOW TO WRITE A BOOK IN 30 DAYS -042
BY Dr. BAK NGUYEN

In HOW TO WRITE YOUR BOOK IN 30 DAYS, Dr. Bak has crafted writing skills and techniques that can be shared and mastered. This book is mainly about structure and how to keep moving forward, avoiding the hit of the INSPIRATION WALL. You will find a wealth of wisdom from his experience writing your first, second, or even 10th book. Dr. Bak is sharing his secrets writing books, having written himself 72 books within 36 months. Visionary businessman, doctor in dentistry, Dr. Bak describes himself as a Dentist by circumstances, a communicator by passion, and an entrepreneur by nature.

HOW TO WRITE A SUCCESSFUL BUSINESS PLAN -049
BY Dr. BAK NGUYEN & ROUBA SAKR

In HOW TO WRITE A SUCCESSFUL BUSINESS PLAN, Dr. Bak is given 20 plus years of experience and knowledge of what it is to be an entrepreneur and more importantly, how to have the investors and banks on your side. Being an entrepreneur is surely not something you learn from school, but there are steps to master so you can communicate your views and vision. That's the only way you will have financing.Writing a business is only not a mandatory stop only for the bankers, but an essential step to every entrepreneur, to know the direction and what's coming next. A business plan is also not set in stone, if there is a truth in business is that nothing will go as planned. Writing down your business plan the first time will prepare you to adapt and to overcome the challenges and surprises. For most entrepreneurs, a business is a passion. To most investors and all banks, a business is a system. Your business plan is the map to that system. However unique your ideas and business are, the mapping follows the same steps and pattern.

HUMILITY FOR SUCCESS -051
BALANCING STRATEGY AND EMOTIONS
BY Dr. BAK NGUYEN

HUMILITY FOR SUCCESS is exploring the emotional discomforts and challenges champions, and overachievers put themselves through. Success is never done overnight and on the way, just like the pain and the struggles aren't enough, we are dealing with the doubts, the haters, and those who like to tell us how to live our lives and what to do. At the same time, nothing of worth can be achieved alone. Every legend has a cast of characters, allies, mentors, companions, rivals, and foes. So one needs the key to social behaviour. HUMILITY FOR SUCCESS is exploring the matter and will help you sort out beliefs from values, peers from friends. Humility is much more about how we see ourselves than how others see us. For any entrepreneur and champion, our daily is to set our mindset right, and to perfect our skills, not to fit in. There is a world where CONFIDENCE grows is in synergy with HUMILITY. As you set the right label on the right belief, you will be able to grow and to leave the lies and haters far behinds. This is HUMILITY FOR SUCCESS.

HYBRID -011
THE MODERN QUEST OF IDENTITY
BY Dr. BAK NGUYEN

IDENTITY -004
THE ANTHOLOGY OF QUESTS
BY Dr. BAK NGUYEN

What if John Lennon was still alive and running for president today? What kind of campaign will he be running? IDENTIFY -THE ANTHOLOGY OF QUESTS is about the quest each of us has to undertake, sooner or later, THE QUEST OF IDENTITY. Citizen of the world, aim to be one, the one, one whole, one unity, made of many. That's the anthology of life! Start with your one, find your unity, and your legend will start. We are all small-minded people anyway! We need each other to be one! We need each other to be happy, so we, so you, so I, can be happy. This is the chorus of life. This is our song! Citizens of the world, I salute you! This is the first tome of the IDENTITY QUEST. FORCES OF NATURE (tome 2) will be following in SUMMER 2021. Also under development, Tome 3 - THE CONQUEROR WITHIN will start production soon.

INDUSTRIES DISRUPTORS -006
BY Dr. BAK NGUYEN

INDUSTRIES DISRUPTORS is a strange title, one that sparkles mixed feelings. A disruptor is someone making a difference, and since we, in general, do not like change, the label is mostly negative. But a disruptor is mostly someone who sees the same problem and challenge from another angle. The disruptor will tackle that angle and come up with something new from something existent. That's evolution! In INDUSTRIES DISRUPTORS, Dr. Bak is joining forces with James Stephan-Usypchuk to share with us what is going on in the minds and shoes of those entrepreneurs disrupting the old habits. Dr. Bak is changing the world from a dental chair, disrupting the dental, and now the book industry. James is a maverick in the Intelligence space, from marketing to Artificial Intelligence. Coming from very different backgrounds and industries, they end up telling very similar stories. If disruptors change the world, well, their story proves that disruptors can be made and forged. Here's the recipe. Here are their stories.

K

KRYPTO -040
TO SAVE THE WORLD
BY Dr. BAK NGUYEN & ILYAS BAKOUCH

L

LEADERSHIP -003
PANDORA'S BOX
BY Dr. BAK NGUYEN

LEADERSHIP, PANDORA'S BOX is 21 presidential speeches for a better tomorrow for all of us. It aims to drive HOPE and motivation into each and every one of us. Together we can make the difference, we hold such power. Covering themes from LOYALTY to GENEROSITY, from FREEDOM and INTELLIGENCE to DOUBTS and DEATH, this is not the typical presidential or motivational speeches that we are used to. LEADERSHIP PANDORA'S BOX will surf your emotions first, only to dive with you to touch the core and soul of our meaning: to matter. This is not a Quest of Identity, but the cry to rally as a species, to raise our heads toward the future, and to move forward as a WHOLE. Not a typical Dr. Bak's book, LEADERSHIP, PANDORA'S BOX is a must-read for all of you looking for hope and purpose, all of us, citizens of the world.

LEVERAGE -014
COMMUNICATION INTO SUCCESS

BY Dr. BAK NGUYEN

In LEVERAGE COMMUNICATION TO SUCCESS, Dr. Bak shares his secret and mindsets to elevate an idea into a vision and a vision into an endeavour. Some endeavours will be a project, some others will become companies, and some will grow into a movement. It does not matter, each started with great communication.Communication is a very vast concept, education, sale, sharing, empowering, coaching, preaching, entertaining. Those are all different kinds of communication. The intent differs, the audiences vary, the messages are unique but the frame can be templated and mastered. In LEVERAGE COMMUNICATION TO SUCCESS, Dr. Bak is loyal to his core, sharing only what he knows best, what he has done himself. This book is dedicated to communicating successfully in business.

MASTERMIND, 7 WAYS INTO THE BIG LEAGUE -052
BY Dr. BAK NGUYEN & JONAS DIOP

MASTERMIND, 7 WAYS INTO THE BIG LEAGUE is the result of the encounter of business coach Jonas Diop and Dr. Bak. As a professional podcaster and someone always seeking the truth and ways to leverage success and performance, coach Jonas is putting Dr. Bak to the test, one that should reveal his secret to overachieve month after month, accumulating a new world record every month. Follow those two great minds as they push each other to surpass themselves, each in their own way and own style. MASTERMIND, 7 WAYS INTO THE BIG LEAGUE is more than a roadmap to success, it is a journey and a live testimony as you are turning the pages, one by one.

MIDAS TOUCH -065
POST-COVID DENTISTRY
BY Dr. BAK NGUYEN, Dr. JULIO REYNAFARJE AND Dr. PAUL OUELLETTE

MIDAS TOUCH, is the memoir of what happened in the ALPHAS SUMMIT in the midst of the GREAT PAUSE as great minds throughout the world in the dental field are coming together. As the time of competition is obsolete, the new era of collaboration is blooming. This is the 3rd book of the ALPHAS, after AFTERMATH and RELEVANCY, all written in the midst of confinement. Dr. Julio Reynafarje is bearing this initiative, to share with you the secret of a successful and lasting relationship with your patients, balancing science and psychology, kindness, and professionalism. He personally invited the ALPHAS to join as co-author, Dr. Paul Ouellette, and Dr. Paul Dominique, and Dr. Bak.Together, they have more than 100 years of combined experience, wisdom, trade, skills, philosophy, and secrets to share with you to empower you in the rebuilding of the dental profession in the aftermath of COVID. RELEVANCY was about coming together and to rebuild the future. MIDAS TOUCH is about how to build, one treatment plan at a time, one story at a time, one smile at a time.

MINDSET ARMORY -050
BY Dr. BAK NGUYEN

MINDSET ARMORY is Dr. Bak's 49th book, days after he completed his world record of writing 48 books within 24 months, on top of being a CEO of Mdex & Co and a full-time cosmetic dentist. Dr. Bak is undoubtedly an OVERACHIEVER. From his last books, he has shared more and more of his lifestyle and how it forged his winning mindset. Within MINDSET ARMORY, Dr. Bak is sharing with us his tools, how he found them, forged them, and leverage them. Just like any warrior needs a shield, a sword, and a ride, here are Dr. Bak's. For any entrepreneur, the road to success is a long and winding journey. On the way, some will find allies and foes. Some allies will become foes, and some foes might become allies. In today's competitive world, the only constant is change. With the right tool, it is possible to achieve. The right tool, the right mindset. This is MINDSET ARMORY.

MIRROR -085
BY Dr. BAK NGUYEN

MIRROR is the theme for a personal book. Not only to Dr. Bak but to all of us looking to reach beyond who and what we actually are. MIRROR is special in the fact that it is not only the content of the book that is of worth but the process in which Dr. Bak shared his own evolution. To go beyond who we are, one must grow every day. And how do you compare your growth and how far have you reach? Looking in the mirror. In all of Dr. Bak's writing, looking at the past is a trap to avoid at all costs. Looking in the mirror, is that any better? Share Dr. Bak's way to push and keep pushing himself without friction nor resistance. Please read that again. To evolve without friction or resistance... that is the source of infinite growth and the unification of the Quest for Power and the Quest of Happiness.

MOMENTUM TRANSFER -009
BY Dr. BAK NGUYEN & Coach DINO MASSON

How to be successful in your business and in your life? Achieve Your Biggest Goals With MOMENTUM TRANSFER. START THE BUSINESS YOU WANT - AND BRING IT NEXT LEVEL! GET THE LIFE YOU ALWAYS WANTED - AND IMPROVE IT! TAKE ANY PROJECTS YOU HAVE - AND MAKE IT THE BEST! In this powerful book, you'll discover what a small business owner learned from a millionaire and successful entrepreneur. He applied his mentor's principles and is explaining them in full detail in this book. The small business owner wrote the book he has always wanted to read and went from the verge of bankruptcy to quadrupling his revenues in less than 9 months and improve his personal life by increasing his energy and bring back peacefulness. Together, the millionaire and the small business owner are sharing their most valuable business and life lessons to the world. The most powerful book to increase your momentum in your business and your life introduces simple and radical life-changing concepts: Multiply your business revenues by finding the Eye of your Momentum - Increase your energy by building and feeding your own Momentum - How to increase your confidence with these simple steps - How to transfer your new powerful energy into other aspects of your business and life - How to set goals and achieve them (even crush them!)- How to always tap into an effortless and limitless force within you- And much, much more!

PLAYBOOK INTRODUCTION -055
BY Dr. BAK NGUYEN

In PLAYBOOK INTRODUCTION, Dr. Bak is open the door to all the newcomers and aspirant entrepreneurs who are looking at where and when to start. Based on questions of two college students wanting to know how to start their entrepreneurial journey, Dr. Bak dives into his experiences to empower the next generation, not about what they should do, but how he, Dr. Bak, would have done it today. This is an important aspect to recognize in the business world, the world has changed since the INFORMATION AGE and the advent of the millenniums into the market. Most matrix and know-how have to be adapted to today's speed and accessibility to the information. We are living at the INFORMATION AGE, this book is the precursor to the ABUNDANCE AGE, at least to those open to embrace the opportunity.

PLAYBOOK INTRODUCTION 2 -056
BY Dr. BAK NGUYEN

In PLAYBOOK INTRODUCTION 2, Dr. Bak continuing the journey to welcome the newcomers and aspirant entrepreneurs looking at where and when to start. If the first volume covers the mindset, the second is covering much more in-depth the concept of debt and leverage. This is an important aspect to recognize in the business world, the world has changed since the INFORMATION AGE and the advent of the millenniums into the market. Most matrix and know-how have to be adapted to today's speed and accessibility to the information. We are living at the INFORMATION AGE, this book is the precursor to the ABUNDANCE AGE, at least to those open to embrace the opportunity.

POWER -043
EMOTIONAL INTELLIGENCE
BY Dr. BAK NGUYEN

IN POWER, EMOTIONAL INTELLIGENCE, Dr. Bak is sharing his experiences and secrets leveraging on his EMOTIONAL INTELLIGENCE, a power we all have within. From SYMPATHY, having others opening up to you, to ACTIVE LISTENING, saving you time and energy; from EMPATHY, allowing you to predict the future to INFLUENCE, enabling you to draft the future, not to forget the power of the crowd with MOMENTUM, you are now in possession of power in tune with nature, yourself. It is a unique take on the subject to empower you to find your powers and your destiny. Visionary businessman, doctor in dentistry, Dr. Bak describes himself as a Dentist by circumstances, a communicator by passion, and an entrepreneur by nature.

POWERPLAY -078
HOW TO BUILD THE PERFECT TEAM
BY Dr. BAK NGUYEN

In POWERPLAY, HOW TO BUILD THE PERFECT TEAM, Dr. Bak is sharing with you his experience, perspective, and mistake traveling the journey of the entrepreneur. A serial entrepreneur himself, he started venture only with a single partner as team to build companies with a director of human resources and a board of directors. POWERPLAY is not a story, it is the HOW TO build the perfect team, knowing that perfection is a lie. So how can one build a team that will empower his or her vision? How to recruit, how to train, how to retain? Those are all legitimate questions. And all of those won't matter if the first question isn't answered: what is the reason for the team? There is the old way to hire and the new way to recruit. Yes, Human Resources is all about mindset too! This journey is one of introspection, of leadership, and a cheat sheet to build, not only the perfect team but the team that will empower your legacy to the next level.

PROFESSION HEALTH - TOME ONE -005
THE UNCONVENTIONAL QUEST OF HAPPINESS
BY Dr. BAK NGUYEN, Dr. MIRJANA SINDOLIC, Dr. ROBERT DURAND AND COLLABORATORS

Why are health professionals burning out while they give the best of themselves to heal the world? Dr. Bak aims to break the curse of isolation that health professionals face and establish a conversation to start the healing process. PROFESSION HEALTH is the basis of an ongoing discussion and will also serve as an introduction to a study lead by Professor Robert Durand, DMD, MSc Science from University of Montreal, study co-financed by Mdex and the Federal Government of Canada. Co-writers are Dr. Mirjana Sindolic, Professor Robert Durand, Dr. Jean De Serres, MD and former President of Hema Quebec, Counsel-Minister Luis Maria Kalaff Sanchez, Dr. Miguel Angel Russo, MD, Banker Anthony Siggia, Banker Kyles Yves, and more...
This is the first Tome of three, dedicated to help "WHITE COATS" to heal and to find their happiness.

REBOOT -012
MIDLIFE CRISIS
BY Dr. BAK NGUYEN

MidLife Crisis is a common theme to each of us as we reach the threshold. As a man, as a woman, why is it that half of the marriages end up in recall? If anything else would have half those rates of failure, the lawsuits would be raining. Where are the flaws, the traps? Love is strong and pure, why is marriage not the reflection of that?

All hard to ask questions with little or no answers. Dr. Bak is sharing his reflections and findings as he reached himself the WALL OF MARRIAGE. This is a matter that affects all of our lives. It is time for some answers.

RELEVANCY - TOME TWO -064
REINVENTING OURSELVES TO SURVIVE
BY Dr. BAK NGUYEN & Dr. PAUL OUELLETTE AND COLLABORATORS

THE GREAT PAUSE was a reboot of all the systems of society. Many outdated systems will not make it back. The Dental Industry is a needed one, it has laid on complacency for far too long. In an age where expertise is global and democratized and can be replaced with technologies and artificial intelligence, the REBOOT will force, not just an update, but an operating system replacement and a firmware upgrade.First, they saved their industry with THE ALPHAS INITIATIVE, sharing their knowledge and vision freely to all the world's dental industry. With the OUELLETTE INITIATIVE, they bought some time to all the dental clinics to resume and to adjust. The warning has been given, the clock is now ticking. who will prevail and prosper and who will be left behind, outdated and obsolete?

RISING -062
TO WIN MORE THAN YOU ARE AFRAID TO LOSE
BY Dr. BAK NGUYEN

In RISING, TO WIN MORE TAN YOU ARE AFRAID TO LOSE, Dr. Bak is breaking down the strategy to success to all, not only those wearing white coats and scrubs. More than his previous book (SUCCESS IS A CHOICE), this one is covering most of the aspects of getting to the next level, psychologically, socially, and financially. Rising is broken down into three key strategies: Financial Leverage - Compressing time - Always being in control. Presented by MILLION DOLLAR MINDSET, the book is covering more than the ways to create wealth, but also how to reach happiness and to live a life without regrets. Dr. Bak the CEO and founder of Mdex & Co, a company with the promise of reforming the whole dental industry for the better. He wrote more than 60 books within 30 months as he is sharing his experiences, secrets, and wisdom.

S

SELFMADE -036
GRATITUDE AND HUMILITY
BY Dr. BAK NGUYEN

This is the story of Dr. Bak, an artist who became a dentist, a dentist who became an Entrepreneur, an Entrepreneur who is seeking to save an entire industry.In his free time, Dr. Bak managed to write 37 books and is a contender to 3 world records to be confirmed. Businessman and visionary, his views and philosophy are ahead of our time. This is his 37th book. In SELFMADE, Dr. Bak is answering the questions most entrepreneurs want to know, the HOWTO and the secret recipes, not just to succeed, but to keep going no matter what! SELFMADE is the perfect read for any entrepreneurs, novices, and veterans.

SUCCESS IS A CHOICE -060
BLUEPRINTS FOR HEALTH PROFESSIONALS
BY Dr. BAK NGUYEN

In SUCCESS IS A CHOICE, FINANCIAL MILLIONAIRE BLUEPRINTS FOR HEALTH PROFESSIONALS, Dr. Bak is breaking down the strategy to success for all those wearing white coats and scrubs: doctors, dentists, pharmacists, chiropractors, nurses, etc. Success is broken down into three key strategies: Financial Leverage - Compressing time - Always being in control. Presented by MILLION DOLLAR MINDSET, the book is covering more than the ways to create wealth, but also how to reach happiness and to live a life without regrets.Dr. Bak is a successful cosmetic dentist with nearly 20 years of experience. He founded Mdex & Co, a company with the promise of reforming the whole dental industry for the better. While doing so, he discovered a passion for writing and for sharing. Multiple times World Record, Dr. Bak is writing a book every 2 weeks for the last 30 months. This is his 60th book, and he is still practicing. How he does it, is what he is sharing with us, SUCCESS, HAPPINESS, and mostly FREEDOM to all Health Professionals.

SYMPHONY OF SKILLS -001
BY Dr. BAK NGUYEN

You will enlighten the world with your potential. I can't wait to see all the differences that you will have in our world. Remember that power comes with responsibility. We can feel in his presence, a genuine force, a depth of energy, confidence, innocence, courage, and intelligence. Bak is always looking for answers, morning and night, he wants to understand the why and the why not. This book is the essence of the man. Dr. Bak is a force of nature who bears proudly his title eHappy. The man never ceases smiling nor spreading his good vibe wherever he passes. He is not trapped in the nostalgia of the past nor the satisfaction of the present, he embodies the joy of what's possible, what's to come. The more we read, the more we share, and we live. That is Bak, he charms us

T

to evolve and to share his points of view, and before we know it, we are walking by his side, a journey we never saw coming.

THE 90 DAYS CHALLENGE -061
BY Dr. BAK NGUYEN

THE 90 DAYS CHALLENGE, is Dr. Bak's journey into the unknown. Overachiever writing 2 books a month on average, for the last 30 months, ambitious CEO, Industries' Disruptor, Dr. Bak seems to have success in everything he touches. Everything except the control of his weight. For nearly 20 years, he struggles with an overweight problem. Every time he scored big, he added on a little more weight. Well, this time, he exposes himself out there, in real-time and without filter, accepting the challenge of his brother-in-law, DON VO to lose 45 pounds within 90 days. That's half a pound a day, for three months. He will have to do so while keeping all of his other challenges on track, writing books at a world record pace, leading the dental industry into the new ERA, and keep seeing his patients. Undoubtedly entertaining, this is the journey of an ALPHA who simply won't give up. But this time, nothing is sure.

THE BOOK OF LEGENDS -024
BY Dr. BAK NGUYEN & WILLIAM BAK

The Book of Legends vol. 1 the story behind the world record of Dr. Bak and his son, William Bak. All Dr. Bak had in mind was to keep his promise of writing a book with his son. They ended up writing 8 children's books within a month, scoring a new world record. William is also the youngest author having published in two languages. Those are world records waiting to be confirmed. History will say: to celebrate a first world record (writing 15 books / 15 months), for the love of his son, he will have scored a second world record: to write 8 books within a month! THE BOOK OF LEGENDS vol. 1 This is both a magical journey for both a father and a son looking to connect and to find themselves. Join Dr. Bak and William Bak in their journey and their love for Life!

THE BOOK OF LEGENDS 2 -041
BY Dr. BAK NGUYEN & WILLIAM BAK

THE BOOK OF LEGENDS vol. 2 is the sequel of "CINDERELLA" but a true story between a father and his son. Together they have discovered a bond and a way to connect. The first BOOK OF LEGENDS covered the time of the first four books they wrote together within a month. The second BOOK OF LEGENDS is covering what happened after the curtains dropped, what happened after reality kicked back in. If the first volume was about a fairy tale in vacation time, the second volume is about making it last in real Life. Share their journey and their love of Life!

THE BOOK OF LEGENDS 3 -086
THE END OF THE INNOCENCE AGE
BY Dr. BAK NGUYEN & WILLIAM BAK

This is the third volume of the series, THE BOOK OF LEGENDS. If the first two happened as a breeze breaking world records on top of world records (27 books written as father and son), the 3rd volume took much more time to arrive. William has grown and writing chicken books is not enough anymore to ignite his imagination. Dr. Bak, as a good father, will try to follow William's growth and invented new games, technics and mind frames to keep engaging William's imagination and interest. From auditions to backstories, Dr. Bak bent backward to keep the adventure going. More than sharing the success and the glory, within THE BOOK OF LEGENDS volume 3, you are sharing the doubts and failure of a father and son refusing to let go... but who have now left MOMENTUM... until the winds blow once more in their favour. Welcome to the Alphas.

THE CONFESSION OF A LAZY OVERACHIEVER -089
REINVENT YOURSELF FROM ANY CRISIS
BY Dr. BAK NGUYEN

In THE CONFESSION OF A LAZY OVERACHIEVER, Dr. Bak is opening up to his new marketing officer, Jamie, fresh out of school. She is young, full of energy, and looking to chill and still to have it all. True to his character, Dr. Bak is giving Jamie some leeway to redefine Dr. Bak's brand to her demographic, the Millennials. This journey is about Dr. Bak satisfying the Millennials and answering their true questions in life. A rebel himself, his ambition to change the world started back on campus, some 25 years ago... then, life caught up with him. It took Dr. Bak 20 years to shake down the burdens of life, to spread his wings free from Conformity, and to start Overachieving. Doctor, CEO, and world record author, here is what Dr. Bak would have love to know 25 years ago as was still on campus. In a word, this is cheating your way to success and freedom. And yes, it is possible. Success, Money, Freedom, it all starts with a mindset and the awareness of Time. Welcome to the Alphas.

THE ENERGY FORMULA -053
BY Dr. BAK NGUYEN

THE ENERGY FORMULA is a book dedicated to help each individual to find the means to reach their purpose and goal in Life. Dr. Bak is a philosopher, a strategist, a business, an artist, and a dentist, how does he do all of that? He is doing so while mentoring proteges and leading the modernization of an entire industry. Until now, Momentum and Speed were the powers that he was building on and from. But those powers come from somewhere too. From a guide of our Quest of Identity, he became an ally in everyone's journey for happiness. THE ENERGY FORMULA is the book revealing step by step, the logic of building the right mindset and the way to ABUNDANCE and HAPPINESS, universally. It is not just a HOW TO book, but one that will change your life and guide you to the path of ABUNDANCE.

THE MODERN WOMAN -070
TO HAVE IT HAVE WITH NO SACRIFICE
BY Dr. BAK NGUYEN & Dr. EMILY LETRAN

In THE MODERN WOMAN: TO HAVE IT ALL WITH NO SACRIFICE, Dr. Bak joins forces with Dr. Emily Letran to empower all women to fulfill their desires, goals, and ambition. Both overachievers going against the odds, they are sharing their experience and wisdom to help all women to find confidence and support to redefine their lives. Dr. Emily Letran is a doctor in dentistry, an entrepreneur, author, and CERTIFIED HIGH-PERFORMANCE coach. For an Asian woman, she made it through the norms and the red tapes to find her voice. As she learned and grew with mentors, today she is sharing her secret with the energy that will motivate all of the female genders to stand for what they deserve. Alpha doctor, Bak is joining his voice and perspective since this is not about gender equality, but about personal empowerment and the quest of Identity of each, man and woman. Once more, Dr. Bak is bringing LEVERAGE and REASON to the new social deal between man and woman. This is not about gender, but about confidence.

THE POWER BEHIND THE ALPHA -008
BY TRANIE VO & Dr. BAK NGUYEN

It's been said by a "great man" that "We are born alone and we die alone." Both men and women proudly repeat those words as wisdom since. I apologize in advance, but what a fat LIE! That's what I learned and discovered in life since my mind and heart got liberated from the burden of scars and the ladders of society. I can have it all, not all at the same time, but I can have everything I put my mind and heart into. Actually, it is not completely true. I can have most of what I and Tranie put our minds into. Together, when we feel like one, there isn't much out of our reach. If I'm the mind, she's the heart; if I'm the Will, she's the means. Synergy is the core of our power.Tranie's aim is always Happiness. In Tranie's definition of life, there are no justifications, no excuses, no tomorrow. For Tranie, Happiness is measured by the minutes of every single day. This is why she's so strong and can heal people around her. That may also be why she doesn't need to talk much, since talking about the past or the future is, in her mind, dimming down the magic of the present, the Now. We both respect and appreciate that we are the whole balancing each other's equation of life, of love, of success. I was the plus and the minus, then I became the multiplication factor and grew into the exponential. And how is Tranie evolving in all of this? She is and always will be the balance. If anything, she is the equal sign of each equation.

THE POWER OF Dr. -066
THE MODERN TITLE OF NOBILITY
BY Dr. BAK NGUYEN, Dr. PAVEL KRASTEV AND COLLABORATORS

In THE POWER OF Dr., independent thinkers mean to exchange ideas. An idea can be very powerful if supported with a great work ethic. Work ethic, isn't that the main fabric of our white coats, scrubs, and title? In an era post-COVID where everything has been rebooted and that the healthcare industry is facing its own fate: to evolve or to be replaced, Dr. Bak and Dr. Pavel reveal the source of their power and their playbook to move forward, ahead.The power we all hold is our resilience and discipline. We put that for years at the service of our profession, from a surgical perspective. Now, we can harness that same power to rewrite the rules, the industry, and our future. Post-COVID, the rules are being rewritten, will you be part of the team or left behind?
"You can be in control!" More than personal growth and a motivational book, THE POWER OF Dr. is an awakening call to the doctor you look at when you graduate, with hope, with honour, with determination.

THE POWER OF YES -010
VOLUME ONE: IMPACT
BY Dr. BAK NGUYEN

In THE POWER OF YES, Dr. Bak is sharing his journey opening up and embracing the world, one day at a time, one ask at a time, one wish at a time. Far from a dare, saying YES allowed Dr. Bak to rewrite his mindsets and to break all the boundaries. This book is not one written a few days or weeks, but the accumulation of a journey for 12 months. The journeys started as Dr. Bak said YES to his producer to go on stage and to speak... That YES opened a world of possibilities. Dr. Bak embraced each and every one of them. 12 months later, he is celebrating the new world record of writing 9 books written over a period of 12 months. To him, it will be a miss, missing the 12 on 12 mark. To the rest of the world, they just saw the birth of a force of nature, the Alpha force. THE POWER OF YES is comprised of all the introduction of the adult books written by Dr. Bak within the first 12 months. Chapter by chapter, you can walk in his footstep seeing and smelling what he has. This is reality literature with a twist of POWER. THE POWER OF YES! Discover your potential and your power. This is the POWER OF YES, volume one. Welcome to the Alphas.

THE POWER OF YES 2 -037
VOLUME TWO: SHAPELESS
BY Dr. BAK NGUYEN

In THE POWER OF YES, volume 2, Dr. Bak is continuing his journey discovering his powers and influence. After 12 months embracing the world saying YES, he rose as an emerging force: he's been recognized as an INDUSTRIES DISRUPTOR, got nominated ERNST AND YOUNG ENTREPRENEUR OF THE YEAR, wrote 9 books within 12 months while launching the most ambitious private endeavour to reform his own industry, the dental field. Contender too many WORLD RECORDS, Dr. Bak is doing all of that in parallel. And yes, he is sleeping his nights and yes, he is writing his book himself, from the screen of his iPhone! Far from satisfied, Dr. Bak missed the mark of writing 12 books within 12 months and everything else is shaping and moving, and could come crumbling down at each turn. Now that Dr. Bak understands his powers, he is looking to test them and to push them to their limits, looking to keep scoring world records while materializing his vision and enterprises. This is the awakening of a Force of Nature looking to change the world for the better while having fun sharing. Welcome to the Alphas.

THE POWER OF YES 3 -046
VOLUME THREE: LIMITLESS
BY Dr. BAK NGUYEN

In THE POWER OF YES, volume 3, the journey of Dr. Bak continues where the last volume left, in front of 300 plus people showing up to his first solo event, a Dr. Bak's event. On stage and in this book, Dr. Bak reveals how 12 months saying YES to everything changed his life... actually, it was 18 months.
From a dentist looking to change the world from a dental chair into a multiple times world record author, the journey of openness is a rendez-vous with Fate. Dr. Bak is sharing almost in real-time his journey, experiences, but above all, his feelings, doubts, and comebacks. From one book to the next, from one journey to the next, follow the adventure of a man looking to find his name, his worth, and his place in the world. Doing so, he is touching people Doing so, he is touching people and initiating their rises. Are you ready for more? Are you ready to meet your Fate and Destiny? Welcome to the Alphas.

THE POWER OF YES 4 -087
VOLUME FOUR: PURPOSE
BY Dr. BAK NGUYEN

In THE POWER OF YES, volume 4, the journey continues days after where the last volume left. After setting the new world record of writing 48 books within 24 months, Dr. Bak is not ready to stop. As volume one covers 12 months of journey, volume 2 covers 6 months. Well, volume 3 covers 4 months. The speed is building up and increasing, steadily. This is volume 4, RISING, after breaking the sound barrier. Dr. Bak has reached a state where he is above most resistance and friction, he is now in a universe of his own, discovering his powers as he walks his journeys. This is no fiction story or wishful thinking, THE POWER OF YES is the journey of Dr. Bak, from one world record to the next, from one book to the next. You too can walk your own legend, you just need to listen to your innersole and to open up to the opportunity. May you get inspiration from the legendary journey of Dr. Bak and find your own Destiny. Welcome to the Alphas.

THE RISE OF THE UNICORN -038
BY Dr. BAK NGUYEN & Dr. JEAN DE SERRES

In THE RISE OF THE UNICORN, Dr. Bak is joining forces with his friend and mentor, Dr. Jean De Serres. Together both men had many achievements in their respective industries, but the advent of eHappyPedia, THE RISE OF THE UNICORN is a personal project dear to both of them: the QUEST OF HAPPINESS and its empowerment. This book is a special one since you are witnessing the conversation between two entrepreneurs looking to change the world by building unique tools and media. Just like any enterprise, the ride is never a smooth one in the park on a beautiful day. But this is about eHappyPedia, it is about happiness, right? So it will happen and with a smile attached to it! The unique value of this book is that you are sharing the ups and downs of the launch of a Unicorn, not just the glory of the fame, but also the doubts and challenges on the way. May it inspire you on your own journey to success and happiness.

THE RISE OF THE UNICORN 2 -076
eHappyPedia
BY Dr. BAK NGUYEN & Dr. JEAN DE SERRES

This is 2 years after starting the first tome. Dr. Bak's brand is picking up, between the accumulation of records and the recognition. eHappyPedia is now hot for a comeback. In THE RISE OF THE UNICORN 2, Dr. Bak is retracing and addressing each of Dr. Jean De Serres' concerns about the weakness of the first version of eHappyPedia and the eHappy movement. This is the sort of the creation and a UNICORN both in finance and in psychology. Never before, you will assist in such daily and decision-making process of a world phenomenon and of a company. Dr. Bak and Dr. De Serres are literally using the process of writing this series of books to plan and to brainstorm the birth of a bluechip. More than an intriguing story, this is the journey of 2 experienced entrepreneurs changing the world.

THE U.A.X STORY -072
THE ULTIMATE AUDIO EXPERIENCE
BY Dr. BAK NGUYEN

This is the story of the ULTIMATE AUDIO EXPERIENCE, U.A.X. Follow Dr. Bak's footstep on how he invented a new way to read and to learn. Dr. Bak brings his experience as a movie producer and a director to elevate the reading experience to another level with entertaining value and make it accessible to everyone, auditive, and visual people alike.

Three years plus of research and development, countless hours of trials and errors, Dr. Bak finally solved his puzzle: having written more than 1.1 million words. The irony is that he does not like to read, he likes audiobooks! U.A.X. finally allowed the opening of Dr. Bak's entire library to a new genre and media. U.A.X. is the new way to learn and enjoy Audiobooks. Made to be entertaining while keeping the self-educational value of a book, U.A.X. will appeal to both auditive and visual people. U.A.X. is the blockbuster of the Audiobooks. The format has already been approved by iTunes, Amazon, Spotify, and all major platforms for global distribution and streaming.

THE VACCINE -077
BY Dr. BAK NGUYEN & WILLIAM BAK

In THE VACCINE, A TALE OF SPIES AND ALIENS, Dr. Bak reprise his role as mentor to William, his 10 years-old son, both as co-author and as doctor. William is living through the COVID war and has accumulated many, many questions. That morning, they got out all at once. From a conversation between father and son, Dr. Bak is making science into words keeping the interest of his son a Saturday morning in bed. William is not just an audience, he is responsible to map the field with his questions. What started as a morning conversation between father and son, became within the next hour, a great project, their 23rd book together. Learn about the virus, vaccination while entertaining your kids.

TIMING - TIME MANAGEMENT ON STEROIDS -074
BY Dr. BAK NGUYEN & WILLIAM BAK

In TIMING, TIME MANAGEMENT ON STEROIDS, Dr. Bak is sharing his secret to keep overachieving, overdelivering while raising the bar higher and higher. We all have 24 hours in a day, so how can some do so much more than others. Dr. Bak is not only sharing his secrets and mindset about time and efficiency, he is literally living his own words as this book is written within his last sprint to set the next world record of writing 100 books within 4 years, with only 31 days to go. With 8 books to write in 31 days, that's a little less than 4 days per book! Share the journey of a man surfing the change and looking to see where is the limit of the human mind, writing. In the meantime, understand his leverage, mindset, and secrets to challenge your own limits and dreams.

TO OVERACHIEVE EVERYTHING BEING LAZY -090
CHEAT YOUR WAY TO SUCCESS
BY Dr. BAK NGUYEN

In TO OVERACHIEVE EVERYTHING BEING LAZY, Dr. Bak retaking his role talking to the millennials, the next generation. If in the first tome of the series LAZY, Dr. Bak addresses the general audience of millennials, especially young women, he is dedicating this tome to the ALPHA amongst the millennials, those aiming for the moon and looking, not only to be happy but to change the world. This is not another take on how to cheat your way to success or how to leverage laziness, but this is the recipe to build overachievers and rainmakers. For the young leaders with ambitions and talent, understanding TIME and ENERGY are crucial from your first steps writing your our legend. If Dr. Bak had the chance to do it all over again, this is how he would do it! Welcome to the Alphas.

TORNADO -067
FORCE OF CHANGE
BY Dr. BAK NGUYEN

In TORNADO - FORCE OF CHANGE Dr. Bak is writing solo. In the midst of the COVID war, change is not a good intention anymore. Change, constant change has become a new reality, a new norm. From somebody who holds the title of Industries' Disruptor, how does he yield change to stay in control? Well, the changes from the COVID war are constant fear and much loss of individual liberty. Some can endure the change, some will ride it. Dr. Bak is sharing his angle of navigating the changes, yielding the improvisations, and to reinvent the goals, the means to stay relevant. From fighting to keep his companies Dr. Bak went on to let go the uncontrollable to embrace the opportunity, he reinvented himself to ride the change and create opportunities from an unprecedented crisis. This is the story of a man refusing to kneel and accept defeat, smiling back at faith to find leverage and hope.

TOUCHSTONE -073
LEVERAGING TODAY'S PSYCHOLOGICAL SMOG
BY Dr. BAK NGUYEN & Dr. KEN SEROTA

TOUCHSTONE, LEVERAGING TODAY'S PSYCHOLOGICAL SMOG is mapping to navigate and to thrive in today's high and constant stress environment. After 40 years in practice, Dr. Serota is concerned about the evolution of the career of health care professionals and the never-ending level of stress. What is stress, what are its effects, damages, and symptoms? If COVID-19 revealed to the world that we are fragile, it also revealed most of the broken and the flaws of our system. For now a century, dentistry has been a champion in depression, Dr.ug addiction, and suicide rate, and the curve is far from flattening. Dr. Bak is sharing his perspective and experience dealing with stress and how to leverage it into a constructive force. From the stress of a doctor with no right to failure to the stress of an entrepreneur never knowing the future, Dr. Bak is sharing his way to use stress as leverage.

ABOUT THE AUTHORS

From Canada, **Dr BAK NGUYEN**, Nominee Ernst and Young Entrepreneur of the year, Grand Homage Lys DIVERSITY, and LinkedIn & TownHall Achiever of the year. Dr Bak is a cosmetic dentist, CEO and founder of Mdex & Co. His company is revolutionizing the dental field. Speaker and motivator, he wrote 72 books over 36 months accumulating many world records (to be officialized).

- **ENTREPRENEURSHIP**
- **LEADERSHIP**
- **QUEST OF IDENTITY**
- **DENTISTRY AND MEDICINE**
- **PARENTING**
- **CHILDREN BOOKS**
- **PHILOSOPHY**

In 2003, he founded Mdex, a dental company upon which in 2018, he launched the most ambitious private endeavour to reform the dental industry, Canada wide. Philosopher, he has close to his heart the quest of happiness of the people surrounding him, patients and colleagues alike. In 2020, he launched an International collaborative initiative named **THE ALPHAS** to share knowledge and for Entrepreneurs and Doctors to thrive through the Greatest Pandemic and Economic depression of our time.

In 2016, he co-found with Tranie Vo, Emotive World Incorporated, a tech research company to use technology to empower happiness and sharing. U.A.X. the ultimate audio experience is the landmark project on which the team is advancing, utilizing the technics of the movie industry and the advancement in ARTIFICIAL INTELLIGENCE to save the book industry and to upgrade the continuing education space.

These projects have allowed Dr Nguyen to attract interests from the international and diplomatic community and he is now the center of a global discussion in the wellbeing and the future of the health profession. It is in that matter that he shares his thoughts and encourages the health community to share their own stories.

"It's not worth it go through it alone! Together, we stand, alone, we fall."

Motivational speaker and serial entrepreneur, philosopher and author, from his own words, Dr Nguyen describes himself as a dentist by circumstances, an entrepreneur by nature and a communicator by passion.

He also holds recognitions from the Canadian Parliament and the Canadian Senate.

www.DrBakNguyen.com

AMAZON - BARNES & NOBLE - APPLE BOOKS - KINDLE
SPOTIFY - APPLE MUSIC

From Canada, **William Bak**, is a 10 years old prodigy. At the age of 8 years old, he co-wrote a series of chicken books with his dad, Dr. Bak. Together, they are changing the world, one mind at a time, writing books for kids. So far, they have 28 books together.

He co-wrote the 11 chicken books in ENGLISH and then, had to translate his own books in FRENCH. This is how he has 22 chicken books. William also co-wrote 2 parenting books with his dad, Dr. Bak, THE BOOK OF LEGENDS volumes 1 and 2. Volume 3 is in production. 2 Vaccine books (French and English) and TIMING, William first Apollo Protocol book.

To promote his books, William embraced the stage for the first time in 2019 talking to a crowd of 300+ people. Since, he has appeared in many videos to talk about his books and upcoming projects.

In the midst of COVID, he got bored and started his YOUTUBE CHANNEL : GAMEBAK, reviewing video games.
By the end of 2020, he has joined THE ALPHAS as the youngest anchor of the upcoming world project COVIDCONOMICS in which he will give his perspective and host the opinions of his generation.

"I will show you. I won't force you. But I won't wait for you.
- William Bak and Dr. Bak

Writing with his Dad, William holds world records to be officialized:

- The youngest author writing in 2 languages
- Co-author of 8 books within a month
- The first kid to have written 20 children books

ULTIMATE AUDIO EXPERIENCE

A new way to learn and enjoy Audiobooks. Made to be entertaining while keeping the self-educational value of a book, UAX will appeal to both auditive and visual people. UAX is the blockbuster of the Audiobooks.

UAX will cover most of Dr Bak's books, and is now negotiating to bring more authors and more titles to the UAX concept. Now streaming on Spotify, Apple Music and available for download on all major music platforms. Give it a try today!

AMAZON - BARNES & NOBLE - APPLE BOOKS - KINDLE
SPOTIFY - APPLE MUSIC

COMBO
PAPERBACK/AUDIOBOOK
ACTIVATION

Please register your book to receive the link to your audiobook version. Register at: https://baknguyen.com/timing-registry

Your license of the audiobook allows you to share with up to 3 peoples the audiobook contained at this link. Book published by Dr. Bak publishing company. Audiobook produced by Emotive World Inc. Copyright 2021, All right reserved.

FROM THE SAME AUTHOR
Dr Bak Nguyen

TITLES AVAILABLE AT
www.DrBakNguyen.com

MAJOR LEAGUES' ACCESS

FACTEUR HUMAIN -035
LE LEADERSHIP DU SUCCÈS
par Dr. BAK NGUYEN & CHRISTIAN TRUDEAU

THE RISE OF THE UNICORN -038
BY Dr. BAK NGUYEN & Dr. JEAN DE SERRES

CHAMPION MINDSET -039
LEARNING TO WIN
BY Dr. BAK NGUYEN & CHRISTOPHE MULUMBA

THE RISE OF THE UNICORN 2 -076
eHappyPedia
BY Dr. BAK NGUYEN & Dr. JEAN DE SERRES

BRANDING -044
BALANCING STRATEGY AND EMOTIONS
BY Dr. BAK NGUYEN

002 - **La Symphonie des Sens**
ENTREPREUNARIAT
par Dr. BAK NGUYEN

006 - **INDUSTRIES DISRUPTORS**
BY Dr .BAK NGUYEN

007 - **Changing the World from a dental chair**
BY Dr. BAK NGUYEN

008 - **The Power Behind the Alpha**
BY TRANIE VO & Dr. BAK NGUYEN

036 - **SELFMADE**
GRATITUDE AND HUMILITY
BY Dr. BAK NGUYEN

072 - **THE U.A.X. STORY**
THE ULTIMATE AUDIO EXPERIENCE
BY Dr. BAK NGUYEN

088 - **CRYPTOCONOMICS 101**
MY PERSONAL JOURNEY
FROM 50K TO 1 MILLION
BY Dr BAK NGUYEN

BUSINESS

SYMPHONY OF SKILLS -001
BY Dr. BAK NGUYEN

CHILDREN'S BOOK
with William Bak

The Trilogy of Legends

THE LEGEND OF THE CHICKEN HEART -016
LA LÉGENDE DU COEUR DE POULET -017
BY Dr. BAK NGUYEN & WILLIAM BAK

THE LEGEND OF THE LION HEART -018
LA LÉGENDE DU COEUR DE LION -019
BY Dr. BAK NGUYEN & WILLIAM BAK

THE LEGEND OF THE DRAGON HEART -020
LA LÉGENDE DU COEUR DE DRAGON -021
BY Dr. BAK NGUYEN & WILLIAM BAK

WE ARE ALL DRAGONS -022
NOUS TOUS, DRAGONS -023
BY Dr. BAK NGUYEN & WILLIAM BAK

The Collection of the Chicken

THE 9 SECRETS OF THE SMART CHICKEN -025
LES 9 SECRETS DU POULET INTELLIGENT -026
BY Dr. BAK NGUYEN & WILLIAM BAK

THE SECRET OF THE FAST CHICKEN -027
LE SECRETS DU POULET RAPIDE -028
BY Dr. BAK NGUYEN & WILLIAM BAK

THE LEGEND OF THE SUPER CHICKEN -029
LA LÉGENDE DU SUPER POULET -030
BY Dr. BAK NGUYEN & WILLIAM BAK

031- **THE STORY OF THE CHICKEN SHIT**
032- **L'HISTOIRE DU CACA DE POULET**
BY Dr. BAK NGUYEN & WILLIAM BAK

033- **WHY CHICKEN CAN'T DREAM?**
034- **POURQUOI LES POULETS NE RÊVENT PAS?**
BY Dr. BAK NGUYEN & WILLIAM BAK

057- **THE STORY OF THE CHICKEN NUGGET**
083- **HISTOIRE DE POULET: LA PÉPITE**
BY Dr. BAK NGUYEN & WILLIAM BAK

082- **CHICKEN FOREVER**
084- **POULET POUR TOUJOURS**
BY Dr BAK NGUYEN & WILLIAM BAK

THE SPIES AND ALIENS COLLECTION

077- **THE VACCINE**
079- **LE VACCIN**
077B- **LA VACUNA**
BY Dr BAK NGUYEN & WILLIAM BAK
TRANSLATION BY BRENDA GARCIA

DENTISTRY

PROFESSION HEALTH - TOME ONE -005
THE UNCONVENTIONAL
QUEST OF HAPPINESS
BY Dr. BAK NGUYEN, Dr. MIRJANA SINDOLIC,
Dr. ROBERT DURAND AND COLLABORATORS

HOW TO NOT FAIL AS A DENTIST -047
BY Dr. BAK NGUYEN

SUCCESS IS A CHOICE -060
BLUEPRINTS FOR HEALTH
PROFESSIONALS
BY Dr. BAK NGUYEN

RELEVANCY - TOME TWO -064
REINVENTING OURSELVES TO SURVIVE
BY Dr. BAK NGUYEN & Dr. PAUL OUELLETTE AND
COLLABORATORS

MIDAS TOUCH -065
POST-COVID DENTISTRY
BY Dr. BAK NGUYEN, Dr. JULIO REYNAFARJE AND
Dr. PAUL OUELLETTE

THE POWER OF DR -066
THE MODERN TITLE OF NOBILITY
BY Dr. BAK NGUYEN, Dr. PAVEL KRASTEV AND
COLLABORATORS

QUEST OF IDENTITY

004- **IDENTITY**
THE ANTHOLOGY OF QUESTS
BY Dr. BAK NGUYEN

011- **HYBRID**
THE MODERN QUEST OF IDENTITY
BY Dr. BAK NGUYEN

LIFESTYLE

045- **HORIZON, BUILDING UP THE VISION**
VOLUME ONE
BY Dr. BAK NGUYEN

048- **HORIZON, ON THE FOOTSTEPS OF TITANS**
VOLUME TWO
BY Dr. BAK NGUYEN

068- **HORIZON, DREAMING OF TRAVELING**
VOLUME THREE
BY Dr. BAK NGUYEN

MILLION DOLLAR MINDSET

MOMENTUM TRANSFER -009
BY Dr. BAK NGUYEN & Coach DINO MASSON

LEVERAGE -014
COMMUNICATION INTO SUCCESS
BY Dr. BAK NGUYEN AND COLLABORATORS

HOW TO WRITE A BOOK IN 30 DAYS -042
BY Dr. BAK NGUYEN

POWER -043
EMOTIONAL INTELLIGENCE
BY Dr. BAK NGUYEN

HOW TO WRITE A SUCCESSFUL BUSINESS PLAN -049
BY Dr BAK NGUYEN & ROUBA SAKR

MINDSET ARMORY -050
BY Dr. BAK NGUYEN

MASTERMIND, 7 WAYS INTO THE BIG LEAGUE -052
BY Dr. BAK NGUYEN & JONAS DIOP

PLAYBOOK INTRODUCTION -055
BY Dr. BAK NGUYEN

PLAYBOOK INTRODUCTION 2 -056
BY Dr. BAK NGUYEN

062- **RISING**
TO WIN MORE THAN YOU ARE AFRAID TO LOSE
BY Dr. BAK NGUYEN

067- **TORNADO**
FORCE OF CHANGE
BY Dr. BAK NGUYEN

071- **BOOTCAMP**
BOOKS TO REWRITE MINDSETS INTO WINNING STATES OF MIND
BY Dr. BAK NGUYEN

074- **TIMING**
TIME MANAGEMENT ON STEROIDS
BY Dr. BAK NGUYEN & WILLIAM BAK

078- **POWERPLAY**
HOW TO BUILD THE PERFECT TEAM
BY Dr. BAK NGUYEN

PARENTING

024- **THE BOOK OF LEGENDS**
BY Dr. BAK NGUYEN & WILLIAM BAK

041- **THE BOOK OF LEGENDS 2**
BY Dr. BAK NGUYEN & WILLIAM BAK

086- **THE BOOK OF LEGENDS 3**
THE END OF THE INNOCENCE AGE
BY Dr. BAK NGUYEN & WILLIAM BAK

PERSONAL GROWTH

REBOOT -012
MIDLIFE CRISIS
BY Dr. BAK NGUYEN

HUMILITY FOR SUCCESS -051
BALANCING STRATEGY AND EMOTIONS
BY Dr. BAK NGUYEN

THE ENERGY FORMULA -053
BY Dr. BAK NGUYEN

AMONGST THE ALPHA -058
BY Dr. BAK NGUYEN & COACH JONAS DIOP

AMONGST THE ALPHA vol.2 -059
ON THE OTHER SIDE
BY Dr. BAK NGUYEN & COACH JONAS DIOP

THE 90 DAYS CHALLENGE -061
BY Dr. BAK NGUYEN

EMPOWERMENT -069
BY Dr BAK NGUYEN

THE MODERN WOMAN -070
TO HAVE IT HAVE WITH NO SACRIFICE
BY Dr. BAK NGUYEN & Dr. EMILY LETRAN

ALPHA LADDERS -075
CAPTAIN OF YOUR DESTINY
BY Dr BAK NGUYEN & JONAS DIOP

080- **1SELF**
REINVENT YOURSELF
FROM ANY CRISIS
BY Dr BAK NGUYEN

THE LAZY FRANCHISE

089- **THE CONFESSION OF
A LAZY OVERACHIEVER**
BY Dr BAK NGUYEN

090- **TO OVERACHIEVE
EVERYTHING BEING LAZY**
CHEAT YOUR WAY TO SUCCESS
BY Dr BAK NGUYEN

PHILOSOPHY

003- **LEADERSHIP** -003
PANDORA'S BOX
BY Dr. BAK NGUYEN

015- **FORCES OF NATURE**
FORGING THE CHARACTER
OF WINNERS
BY Dr BAK NGUYEN

KRYPTO -040
TO SAVE THE WORLD
BY Dr. BAK NGUYEN & ILYAS BAKOUCH

ALPHA LADDERS 2 -081
SHAPING LEADERS AND ACHIEVERS
BY Dr BAK NGUYEN & BRENDA GARCIA

MIRROR -085
BY Dr BAK NGUYEN

098 - **376 POWER QUOTES**
SHORTCUT VOLUME SIX
BY Dr. BAK NGUYEN

099 - **306 HAPPINESS QUOTES**
SHORTCUT VOLUME SEVEN
BY Dr. BAK NGUYEN

100 - **170 DOCTOR QUOTES**
SHORTCUT VOLUME EIGHT
BY Dr. BAK NGUYEN

SHORTCUT

SOCIETY

408 HEALING QUOTES -093
SHORTCUT VOLUME ONE
BY Dr. BAK NGUYEN

408 GROWTH QUOTES -094
SHORTCUT VOLUME TWO
BY Dr. BAK NGUYEN

365 LEADERSHIP QUOTES -095
SHORTCUT VOLUME THREE
BY Dr. BAK NGUYEN

518 CONFIDENCE QUOTES -096
SHORTCUT VOLUME FOUR
BY Dr. BAK NGUYEN

317 SUCCESS QUOTES -097
SHORTCUT VOLUME FIVE
BY Dr. BAK NGUYEN

013 - **LE RÊVE CANADIEN**
D'IMMIGRANT À MILLIONNAIRE
par DR BAK NGUYEN

054 - **CHOC**
LE JARDIN D'EDITH
par DR BAK NGUYEN

063 - **AFTERMATH**
BUSINESS AFTER THE GREAT PAUSE
BY Dr BAK NGUYEN & Dr ERIC LACOSTE

073 - **TOUCHSTONE**
LEVERAGING TODAY'S
PSYCHOLOGICAL SMOG
BY Dr BAK NGUYEN & Dr KEN SEROTA

TO COME - **COVIDCONOMICS**
THE GENERATION AHEAD
BY Dr BAK NGUYEN

THE POWER OF YES

THE POWER OF YES - 010
VOLUME ONE: IMPACT
BY Dr BAK NGUYEN

THE POWER OF YES 2 - 037
VOLUME TWO: SHAPELESS
BY Dr BAK NGUYEN

046 - **THE POWER OF YES 3**
VOLUME THREE: LIMITLESS
BY Dr BAK NGUYEN

087 - **THE POWER OF YES 4**
VOLUME FOUR: PURPOSE
BY Dr BAK NGUYEN

091 - **THE POWER OF YES 5**
VOLUME FIVE: ALPHA
BY Dr BAK NGUYEN

092 - **THE POWER OF YES 6**
VOLUME SIX: PERSPECTIVE
BY Dr BAK NGUYEN

www.DrBakNguyen.com

AMAZON - BARNES & NOBLE - APPLE BOOKS - KINDLE
SPOTIFY - APPLE MUSIC

www.ingramcontent.com/pod-product-compliance
Lightning Source LLC
Chambersburg PA
CBHW071232170426
43191CB00032B/1359